Pursuing Excellence

Pursuing Excellence
A Values-Based, Systems Approach to Help Companies Become More Resilient

Brian Strobel

Routledge
Taylor & Francis Group
A PRODUCTIVITY PRESS BOOK

First published 2021
by Routledge
600 Broken Sound Parkway #300, Boca Raton FL, 33487

and by Routledge
2 Park Square, Milton Park, Abingdon, Oxon, OX14 4RN

Routledge is an imprint of the Taylor & Francis Group, an informa business

© 2021 Taylor & Francis

ISBN: 978-0-367-90304-6 (hbk)
ISBN: 978-0-367-61777-6 (pbk)
ISBN: 978-1-003-02406-4 (ebk)

Typeset in Minion
by codeMantra

For Chiaumey. Thank you for your understanding and forgiveness over the many precious hours I spent away from you while finishing this work. You remain my muse—the reason and cause for everything good that I have come to cherish.

Contents

PART I   Things That Are and That Could Be

PART II   Things We Don't See

PART V   Why These Things Matter

Foreword

In 1964, in the case of *Jacobellis v. Ohio* before the Supreme Court of the United States, Justice Potter Stewart was asked to describe the threshold test for "obscenity." Stewart wrote that he could not define or adequately describe that which is obscene, but he knew it when he saw it. The same might be said of "excellence."

It's a powerful word. It is a word that can elate us, cause us to celebrate others, motivate us to press further, stiffen our spine when we need greater resolve, or help us rally around a cause greater than ourselves. Whether a parent, student, athlete, employee, employer, or a business leader, we all want to achieve excellence and to help others achieve their excellence.

Yet it is a word that is difficult to define—often just a notion. But like Justice Stewart, we know it when we see it.

We see it in sports when the underdog comes from behind to win. We see it in our children when they work hard to achieve personal greatness. We see it in our leaders who are often at their best when things are at their very worst, as we're all too familiar with now in the wake of the COVID-19 pandemic.

Brian Strobel knows excellence when he sees it. From his time as an officer in the US Marine Corps, a high-performance organization that relentlessly pursues excellence, Strobel was immersed in a culture of excellence every day. As a result, he probably recognizes excellence more by its absence than by its presence.

In *Pursuing Excellence*, Strobel walks us through what excellence looks like; its values and beliefs, culture, leadership and strategy, systems and structures, marketspace, people, processes, products, and the customer experience. He is not too shy to make a special call-out for the need to achieve sustainable profit. His construct for this book serves as a series of waypoints for the journey on which Strobel will take the reader, walking through each on its own and as a part of the whole. And he shares his definition of excellence that serves as the lighthouse throughout the book.

Readers will gain an understanding that *Pursuing Excellence* is a book about organizational design: how to get a company to operate better as a values-based organization; not just vertical optimizations but horizontal integrations as well. It will become unmistakable that becoming a high-performance organization starts with high-performance individuals working in high-performance teams and having a culture of leadership in which people can thrive. And through which their goals can be realized.

Although the subject matter is serious, Strobel takes the reader on the journey by sharing stories from his life and examples from his experiences as a Marine and as a corporate leader, sharing instances where there was excellence and also where there was not. This makes *Pursuing Excellence* an easy, enjoyable, and relatable read.

This book doesn't provide any detailed formula. Strobel recognizes that companies operate under a variety of circumstances, with different priorities, and work from different places in their business cycle. Instead, he provides a roadmap that guides you through the things that are important, regardless of where you are, and leaves it up to you to fill in the blanks, allowing the reader to decide on the details.

If we want to become the best versions of ourselves and be part of organizations that are the best versions of themselves in our new world, then we need to be "pursuing excellence."

Joseph F. Paris Jr.
Founder, Operational Excellence Society
Author of State of Readiness

Acknowledgments

I developed the concept for this work six years ago. I completed most of the first draft just before the World Health Organization declared the coronavirus a pandemic. While this book's ideas have nothing to do with our current situation, they may also have everything to do with it.

Just like 9/11 changed the world, we're experiencing another event that will forever change our core beliefs, but on a much larger scale. This book doesn't focus on that critical issue, but it does provide ideas for our companies to operate more efficiently and become more resilient. And it does so while helping ensure they focus on the right things. Our current state will only exasperate this need.

Far more people than I can list here have contributed to this effort. I'm indebted to those authors, thinkers, and organizational leaders who developed concepts that I've leveraged and transformed to convey the ideas presented in this work. I've attempted to deliver truths through building upon these earlier discoveries and coalescing them into this singular idea of Operational Excellence.

As many of my concepts leverage from others, I've directly cited those instances where the original words best communicate the ideas under discussion. Some models in the text are my personal development. Others are derivatives of common models I've transformed into Operational Excellence applications. When leveraging from others, I've given the original thinkers full credit.

Special credit is due to Robert Quinn and John Rohrbaugh for the Competing Values Framework (CVF) that has become foundational to my thinking and the ideas of this book.

The definitions for *"excellence"* and *"organizational excellence"* are reprinted with permission from ASQ, *www.asq.org*. All rights reserved. No further distribution allowed without permission.

My CVF and Organizational Culture Assessment Instrument (OCAI) figures are adapted with permission from *Diagnosing and Changing Organizational Culture* by Kim S. Cameron and Robert Quinn, published by Jossey-Bass. Copyright © 2011 by John Wiley & Sons, Inc. All rights reserved.

The definition of culture is from *Organizational Culture and Leadership* by Edgar H. Schein, published by John Wiley & Sons, Inc. and is used with permission. Copyright © 2017 by Edgar H. Schein. All rights reserved.

The ISO Quality Management Principles ©ISO are excerpted from ISO's "Quality Management Principles" with permission of the American National Standards Institute (ANSI) on behalf of the International Organization for Standardization. All rights reserved.

Merriam-Webster Collegiate Dictionary and Thesaurus Online available at *http://merriam-webster.com/dictionary* provides all dictionary definitions used throughout the text.

I've drawn additional content material from my articles previously published on LinkedIn. These include *Clarifying Your Written Intent*; *Leading as a Servant*; *The Normalization of Deviance*; *The Case for Operational Excellence*; *Is Your Job Emotionally Barren*; *The Business Mantra of Marcus Lemonis*; and *Leader vs. Manager: A Different Perspective*.

This book draws from my previously published work, *Leading Change from Within*, published by WestBow Press in 2015. I've freely used my earlier ideas and words without further reference.

This work is the culminating effort of nearly 30 years of leading people towards higher performance. I'm thankful for everyone that I've worked with over these many years. You have each helped me become a better man and servant to those I've had to pleasure to lead.

Prologue

This book focuses on how private sector companies can move from average to excellent. It provides an approach to Operational Excellence that can help them become more resilient. My Operational Excellence definition discusses *profit*, something not relevant to the public sector and government. But other concepts inherent to Operational Excellence unquestionably apply to government operations.

It's easy to identify public agencies falling far short of excellence. Examples include FEMA's actions in 2005 surrounding Hurricane Katrina, the 2012 GSA scandal in Las Vegas, or arguably, the government's initial response to the coronavirus. It's more challenging to identify excellence. But if we look, we'll find its presence everywhere. Let's consider an example from the Department of Defense.

Navy Carrier Strike Groups participate in a training exercise before each deployment. The purpose is to certify readiness to conduct military operations at sea and project power ashore. The month-long exercise involves more than 10,000 uniformed men and women, multiple warships, and more than 100 combat aircraft. I had the opportunity to participate in several of these exercises, first as an air wing participant and later as a member of the admiral's staff and evaluator of aviation readiness.

As a participant, my focus was doing my job to the best of my ability. I was responsible for hundreds of Marines that were each responsible for scores of specific operations. My job was to ensure we completed the tasks needed to meet our larger unit's objectives. There were hundreds of leaders in similar roles to mine, each with comparable duties. The collective whole was a fully integrated strike group capable of executing its mission with excellence.

As an evaluator, my aperture expanded. I led a management team chartered to help ensure combat readiness for this incredible fighting arm of the US military. After completing one of these week-long evaluations, I stood outside the carrier's red-lit bridge and its amazing bustle of activity, awaiting my scheduled time to brief the Captain.

While waiting, I watched the world's most advanced military aircraft slam into the flight deck and snag the arresting wire. Other aircraft, assisted by the ship's powerful steam catapult, launched off into the night sky. And throughout these operations, the Captain and his crew continuously repositioned the carrier to ensure favorable winds across the flight deck.

The Chief advised me not to stop briefing until complete, no matter how many times the Captain was pulled to other tasks. My brief lasted 20 minutes. I highlighted findings and actions the crew would need to take to help ensure their readiness. As I was briefing, I watched the Captain provide commands that were each repeated back by sailors prior to executing their orders. They then instinctively acknowledged their action back to the Captain for closure.

Throughout this event, the Captain was advised of flight operations by the Air Boss, of the ship's position by the Navigator, and of the weather by the Officer of the Deck. He was multi-tasking at an unbelievable level. When I finished, he asked several clarifying questions, indicating he heard and fully understood my briefing.

While on the bridge, I saw orders given, taken, and executed with extreme precision. I saw complete alignment, from the Battle Group Commander to the Captain to his officers and staff. I saw complexity managed with flawless agility. I saw risks managed and critical decisions made without hesitation. I saw leaders using systems thinking to understand complexities and interdependencies. I saw the embodiment of accountability, empowerment, and engagement. I had just observed Operational Excellence in action.

In those 45 minutes, I witnessed events that happen every hour of every day across the world's seas aboard these floating cities. I saw people that consistently execute their mission with extreme precision—with excellence. I'm glad these men and women have no interest in *profit*. And I'm grateful for what they do, and for how they do it, to continue keeping our world a safer place.

Introduction

A STORY FROM THE PAST

I remember the day like it was yesterday. It was a Friday morning, almost ten years ago now. I followed my usual routine—pour a cup of coffee, review emails, print my calendar, and schedule my priorities for the day. Most days started the same. And that one was no different.

I had been in my leadership position for several months. The company lost millions of dollars the previous year. A general recognition existed among leadership that "the way things get done around here" needed to change.

I was hired to help develop and deliver that change solution. During my interview, the new president advised the team I would inherit wasn't necessarily the team I would need going forward. Soon I would learn a lot more than just that my team needed to change.

The company was on the path to turning around poor performance and improving the bottom line. But to be clear, this wasn't the triple bottom line. Our accomplishments were coming at a price. Those in the close fight weren't noticing, but I had seen enough to understand decisions focused exclusively on short-term benefits without consideration for longer-term consequences.

I revisited several of the many emails received yesterday. Five of them were particularly concerning:

8:14 am: The VP of Programs advised of difficulty closing contract negotiations with an important customer. He accused the customer of being an idiot for not accepting our terms. I had a different perspective for why negotiations were stalling.

9:46 am: The Director of Compliance provided an email with ten attachments—each one a 15-plus page policy that needed reviewed and then approved or rejected within five days.

11:17 am: The Manufacturing Director advised of part shortages shutting down the production line. He blamed Procurement. I noticed Procurement wasn't included in the email, and he failed to mention his team's planning errors that helped lead to the issue.

12:40 pm: The HR Director requested a meeting to discuss a grievance by our local union for failure to properly distribute work. I noted the scheduled time conflicted with a previously scheduled event already on my calendar.

3:47 pm: The VP of Engineering sent a meeting notice with the subject "Internal R&D is Broken!" The text discussed R&D funding concerns. Her meeting request conflicted with the day and time HR chose for the grievance discussion.

I would need to deal with each of these in the coming days. But for now, my focus was on the morning schedule. My agenda was typical. I was destined to spend most of the day in a series of poorly run meetings that would struggle to make difficult decisions or resolve important issues.

The Industrial Engineering group organized my first meeting—a kaizen event held on the production floor. The engineers were conducting a time study of manufacturing employees to reduce labor costs. The intent was to record the time needed to complete tasks and then remove waste from the process. If successful, they hoped to cut several minutes from the manufacturing flow.

On my way to the event, I passed a group of employees having a casual conversation near a large grinding machine. The grinder was making parts for the customer we were struggling with on negotiations. I gently reminded them to put on their hearing protection. At first, they didn't hear me, as the grinder was particularly loud that day. I asked again, and they grudgingly complied.

I arrived at the kaizen just as the time study kicked off. There I watched a disengaged employee, Bob, perform his tasks using a tool that didn't seem to be designed for the job. He was pretending to follow instructions he obviously didn't believe were appropriate for the task.

The instructions were written by an engineer who didn't fully understand the product, process, or strategy. He tended to counter this ignorance by writing complicated procedures that most of us, including Bob, struggled to understand.

Throughout the event, Bob kept a nervous eye on his supervisor, whom he didn't trust. Always concerned about his employment stability and our increasing demand for efficiency, Bob understood the importance of faking interest. The industrial engineers were excited and openly discussing potential KPI reductions. Bob wasn't sure what that meant, or even what the acronym KPI meant, but he knew enough to pretend that he cared.

We finished two hours later. The engineers considered the event a major success. They shaved 14 minutes of waste from the time allocated to complete the tasks. The KPI targets could now be revised to lower planned labor hours. Management was going to be pleased. I left the scene with mixed emotions.

The Procurement Director stopped me on the way to my next meeting. He needed help with a situation that violated common sense. One of his best employees had just resigned. A mother with young children, she requested a schedule adjustment to allow her to work from home several days a week. Human Resources denied the request. The decision conflicted with what she valued, so she chose to resign.

She was probably our most efficient buyer. She was definitely our most driven buyer. Her job required at least 50 percent travel, so she already found a way to be productive without physically being in the office. But the company wasn't ready to set a precedent and allow employees to work from home.

The procurement organization wasn't within my responsibilities, but the director knew I viewed these things through a different lens. I told him I would raise the issue with the president. I honestly didn't think I could change the decision, but someone needed to try.

I stopped by my assistant's desk on the way to my next meeting. I had just been requested for three more meetings. We could delay two of them, but one was a three-hour session with the president. My assistant would need to rearrange my calendar and further delay several important discussions. Engineering canceled the much-anticipated R&D meeting, so that freed up some time. The project had suffered more budget cuts and now couldn't even fund this planning meeting.

My next event was a resource planning review in the large boardroom. Walking to the boardroom, I mentally rescheduled my priorities. The meeting was starting in less than a minute. A manager on my team was coming down the hall opposite me. He stopped, inverted his direction, and walked with me. He appeared anxious and needed help on a decision.

I listened to his concerns as we walked, still mentally shuffling my priorities. The previous meeting hadn't yet adjourned by the time we reached the boardroom.

The manager pressed me for a decision. My delay was partly due to my mental multitasking and partly due to frustration from his inaction. The decision was clearly within his authority, yet he either didn't feel empowered to do so or couldn't see the obvious path to resolution.

Rather than make the decision, I asked him to see me at the end of the day. By then, I would have more time so we could review our RACI matrix and walk through our delegation authority. Hopefully, with this additional coaching, he could arrive at the decision himself.

But he pressed. The issue was now at critical mass and delaying delivery of a large order. It had festered for weeks and demanded immediate action. I decided for him, noting that we would still keep our end-of-day meeting to review how he could have better handled the situation.

Engaged with the manager, I hadn't noticed we were still delayed access to the boardroom. The previous group was over their time by 20 minutes. Nine people were outside waiting for the last meeting to end. Nine people multiplied by 20 minutes—that's three full labor hours. Each were managers making much more than Bob. We were excited about the 14 minutes we saved Bob from this morning, but somehow freely tolerated waste in our management process.

I entered the boardroom and requested the group readjourn to a different location. Our resource planning review was too important to delay any further.

Our meeting started 25 minutes late. Of the nine people present, none were from Programs or Business Development. The Operations arm could plan all it wanted, but without insight to the upcoming requirements, our planning efforts would be futile. We discussed process for 20 minutes and then adjourned.

Throughout the remainder of the day, I participated in a series of management reviews. Each one analyzed our performance over the last 30 days. The analysis was excruciating. The process, like the rejection for the work from home request, violated common sense.

The leadership team, all highly compensated, would often spend hours trying to remove minutes from hourly employee tasks. We were failing to grasp the larger picture. We somehow believed any improvement, without consideration for the impact on morale, employee engagement or the effort needed to achieve it, was how we should focus our energy.

The process was exhausting. The product from this effort was a long list of action items intended to correct performance. These included formalizing cost reductions from the morning kaizen event.

Later that afternoon, after meeting with the manager as promised, I sat alone in my office and reflected on the day. Things weren't supposed to be this way. We were a Fortune 500 company. We employed smart people and maintained a decent reputation in our industry. We even had a dedicated continuous improvement team. But was I the only one that could see what was happening?

We were obsessed with analyzing every historical nuance of operational performance, continually looking for ways to drive improvements to factory efficiency. But we struggled with inefficiencies from poor engagement that kept us far below optimum performance levels. The friction present in our daily routine was almost overwhelming. And the products of our improvement efforts had plateaued and weren't enabling us to move to the next level.

Our focus was exclusively on the rear-view mirror. I was growing increasingly concerned about who, if anyone, was looking forward to watch where we were going. While we focused on driving costs out of the business, our competitors were developing innovative technologies to awe our customers and lure them away from our products. And we didn't seem to notice.

We needed to change our mindset. We needed a different strategy. And we needed it now.

Our company, like so many others seeking improvement, focused its improvement efforts on the concepts of Lean and Six Sigma. But without an integrated solution, these will fail to transform the business. Early in my role, I conducted several cultural assessments across our organization. These confirmed stability and control dominated our cultural focus. We placed little emphasis on agility and freedom of action.

We spent every moment focusing inward. And our approach to continuous improvement enhanced this flaw. We were in dire need of a new solution—a complete solution. Borrowing from what I had done in other organizations, I began to develop our plan to pursue excellence.

APPLYING THE BOOK'S CONCEPTS

To pursue Operational Excellence is to invite change—and not just any change. We're not talking about adjusting what *is*—we're talking about creating what *isn't*. A commitment here, which executive leadership must champion, is a commitment to deliver end-to-end business transformation.

A company doesn't *implement* Operational Excellence as a methodology, model, or tool. Instead, a company *realizes* Operational Excellence. It does so by integrating effective leadership, teamwork, problem-solving, systems thinking, and continuous improvement. It *achieves* this by aligning strategies, empowering employees, optimizing business processes, and improving the customer experience.

Our companies are searching for more. What was good enough last year will now deliver us somewhere short of average. While there is no panacea, not having a plan is a sure path to irrelevance.

As you read this work, I'll ask that you prepare to unlearn some things. Many of the general discussions won't be groundbreaking. On the contrary, most elements are proven concepts within their specific field. This book brings together best practices and new ideas in a single work that takes a systems approach and demonstrates a compelling path to achieve excellence.

The book is intended for leaders who are seeking to move their companies from average to excellent. The work is framed to help them do so in our new business environment that has yet to fully reveal its final state. It's for those companies seeking to move beyond the actions that address conformity to a standard to one that addresses our needs on this journey to excellence.

There are other paths to help our companies improve their performance. We have the ISO family of standards that, as we'll discuss later, help us achieve average and conforming performance. And we have the Baldrige Award, which *is* based on excellence, but which also comes through a heavy investment in government-mandated criteria that may distract us from our focus on the customer.

This book provides an alternative solution.

I'm offering a solution based on common leadership and management principles. This work departs from other books on Operational Excellence. It's not presented in Lean speak or corporate speak. It's presented in everyday language common to leaders and managers.

As we move forward together in our new world as it has become, our companies must change to survive. The ideas presented here can be implemented organically by most companies. Many consulting firms now specialize in Operational Excellence deployment. This doesn't always provide the best solution. Some consultants are exceptional at what they do, but their use can become a crutch and hold a company back from learning and self-sustainment.

A business must never outsource its eyes. Michelangelo, da Vinci, and Picasso didn't create their masterpieces through a description by others. They completed their works from their own perspectives, and through their own eyes. The vision for this journey is through the eyes of the leaders within our companies. If external consultants are needed, the best approach may be one that uses them in combination with internal members to leverage the respective strengths of each perspective.

Pursuing Excellence is a leadership book. I'm not going to discuss improved approaches to kaizen, gemba, or kanban. I am going to discuss how our companies, through a values-based system approach, can take the proceeds from these tactical efforts to realize long-term, transformational improvement.

The discussion doesn't provide direction "to do it this way." Rather, the book culls ideas from hundreds of leadership and management books, theories, and models. It combines these with my learning from advanced education and certifications plus 30 years of leading people in operational environments within the public and private sectors. I've coalesced these different ideas and experiences to present concepts intended to stimulate thoughts within the reader of just what may be possible.

And I want to emphasize that this is a simple book: an easy-to-read essay intended to be finished in a few short sittings. While one could argue the content as complex, I chose a common-sense presentation over a technical approach. My earlier books contained hundreds of endnotes from extensive bibliographies. This one has far less notes and only a few references. That was intentional.

For this work, I started with the end in mind. I'm seeking to improve the reader's experience while providing a roadmap that can help companies move from average to excellent—to achieve Operational Excellence. And I attempt this not by explaining *how to do* these things, but by providing the stimulant to change *how we think* about these things.

THE LENS OF OPERATIONAL EXCELLENCE

Some of the previous ways that we've managed our companies must change. The world is now a new place, with new rules. Succeeding will require new ways of looking at our problems. The lens of Operational Excellence, shown below, can help us view these things from a different perspective.

A lens is something that bends and refracts light to alter our vision. It allows us to see things differently. The right kind of lens takes what's already there, and through convergence and divergence, provides a different perspective to view the subject. It focuses our vision on those things we need to see with more clarity.

The book's flow follows the construct of this lens. The lens begins each of the book's five parts, representing those *things* that must be understood and embraced to achieve excellence. Discussion delivers the surrounding context *why* each is important to the pursuit of excellence. The lens helps guide our vision towards becoming more resilient by moving closer to achieving excellence.

Part I

Things That Are and That Could Be

Work, as we know it, is becoming a different place. And yet many things remain the same.

Or maybe that's an understatement. Maybe nothing's new.

Twenty-five hundred years ago, King Solomon wrote that which has been is that which shall be.

So why now does everything seem to be changing so fast?

1

Start with the Beginning but Focus on the End

A VERY BRIEF HISTORY OF EXCELLENCE

No one owns the word *excellence*, though some have tried.

According to the United States Patent and Trademark Office, people sought to trademark "excellence" more than 5,000 times over the last 50 years. "A Commitment to Excellence" was first trademarked in 1974 by a heating equipment manufacturer. Al Davis, the longtime owner of the Oakland Raiders, registered his "Commitment to Excellence" trademark in 2002, stating its business use back to 1963.

Quotes intended to inspire us through this idea of "excellence" supposedly exist as far back as Aristotle's time. Vince Lombardi motivated his players by explaining they couldn't attain perfection, but they could catch excellence. The US Air Force created its *Organizational Excellence Award* in 1969. And Peters and Waterman's best-selling and controversial *In Search of Excellence* was published in 1982.

It took the quality community a little longer to catch on.

As we moved into the 80s, Japan was becoming an economic powerhouse on a path to domination. They began recognizing their best companies and their commitment to quality with the Deming Prize in 1951. In response to Japan's rise, the United States countered by creating the *Malcolm Baldrige National Quality Award* in 1987. Not to be outdone, Europe established its European Foundation for Quality Management (EFQM) two years later. Soon after forming, EFQM developed its *Excellence Model*.

The American Society for Quality (ASQ) watched this movement to excellence before acting. Founded in 1946, ASQ began certifying people in quality competencies in 1968. But it wasn't until 2006 that they added *Organizational Excellence* (OE) to the title of their quality manager certification (CMQ-OE). And the US government eventually got on board by renaming the *Malcolm Baldrige National Quality Award* to the *Baldrige Performance Excellence Program* in 2010.

The movement now has complete momentum. And it's global. We should expect interest in this idea of excellence to increase in our new world. The Business Excellence Institute, founded in 2013, claims membership in more than 30 countries across six continents. They maintain their excellence hall of fame and an excellence manifesto that business leaders can endorse to support the movement.

Organizations across the globe are now using *excellence* everywhere. People have excellence within their titles, from technician to chief excellence officer. Centers of Excellence (CoE) are now a basic organizational element across many industries, public and private. These CoE are designed to help us get better at everything, from deploying an armored division to making the perfect Big Mac. Here I refer to the Army's Maneuver Center of Excellence and the Center of Training Excellence at McDonald's Hamburger University.

I'm also part of this trend. I've created Operational Excellence departments to help lead transformation in each of the companies that I've served. And I expect an increased need for such departments within our companies as we look for ways to start doing things differently in our new world.

At this point, we should define excellence. The dictionary doesn't suffice with its definition "the quality of being very good." ASQ provides a better definition with "Excellence is a measure of consistently superior performance that surpasses requirements and expectations without demonstrating significant flaws or waste."

We often place words around excellence. In addition to CoE, we have *Business Excellence, Process Excellence, Execution Excellence, Sustainment Excellence, Organizational Excellence,* and *Operational Excellence,* to name just a few.

Organizational Excellence is the term preferred by ASQ, which they define as

The ongoing efforts to establish an internal framework of standards and processes intended to engage and motivate employees to deliver products and services that fulfill customer requirements within business expectations. It is the achievement by an organization of consistent superior performance...

I think this definition may place too much emphasis on quality. While quality is critically important, such an approach could detract from other essential ideas and functions necessary for us to achieve a state of excellence.

I prefer *Operational Excellence*, defined as *the readiness level achieved when a business becomes aligned in its strategy and the culture is committed to the continuous improvement of performance and the environment of those accomplishing the work. Realizing Operational Excellence results in a more resilient business capable of executing strategy better than competitors, with higher revenues, lower risk, and optimized operating costs.*

This is admittedly a complex definition with multiple interactions. Attempts to reduce it to something simpler miss the essence of what we're trying to accomplish. Whether it's *Operational Excellence* or *Organizational Excellence* or just *excellence*, we're talking about the same thing. But as we're about to see, I believe words to be important.

We need the same understanding of words to arrive at the same place for what we're discussing. But in this case, the discussion obviates the differences. We're talking about how companies improve holistically to achieve this desired state of excellence.

Throughout this writing, I'll use Operational Excellence, and often just excellence. Some abbreviate this as OPEX and others as OE. But we're talking about the same thing. So, let's go ahead and start to unravel how this all relates.

QUALITY MANAGEMENT PRINCIPLES

With this global activity transitioning from quality to excellence, it's interesting to see what the world's leading quality certification body says about excellence. The International Organization for Standardization

(ISO) is the world's largest producer of International Standards. ISO has published more than 22,000 standards that provide voluntary requirements that help define goodness for nearly every aspect of technology and business.

The ISO standard for quality management is the one most people are familiar with and the most popular standard to which companies seek certification. More than one million companies across 170 countries are certified to the ISO 9001 Quality Management Systems standard. Many may be surprised that ISO doesn't use the term *excellence* <u>anywhere</u> within this standard. They don't—go ahead and check.

But ISO does provide a different document, *Quality Management Principles*, which identifies seven principles as best practices for performance improvement. This latter document identifies next steps for how these principles "can form a basis for performance improvement and organizational excellence." The principles, ISO relates, are "a set of fundamental beliefs, norms, rules and values that are accepted as true." The seven ISO *Quality Management Principles* are as follows:

Customer focus	Improvement
Leadership	Evidence-based decision-making
Engagement of people	Relationship management
Process approach	

The fact that ISO has identified these principles, aligned with excellence, could indicate they're preparing for an excellence certification soon. I'll discuss why that would be a bad idea at the end of this book. But I don't advise jumping ahead. We'll need to take this journey in stride to understand why *certifying* an organization to excellence would be the wrong path.

An ISO certification establishes minimum standards—or average performance. Companies once sought certification as a discriminator, but it no longer differentiates them from the competition. Being average is no longer good enough.

In today's marketspace, we need to move beyond average to survive in a world of increased competition, continual change, and our new realities of volatility and ambiguity. The best companies are seeking different results. The best companies are now seeking excellence.

CONTINUOUS IMPROVEMENT

There's no panacea for today's business challenges. Some people spend a great deal of time trying to convince us of the benefits available from the latest shiny object. We shouldn't believe the hype.

Prior to the coronavirus pandemic, our businesses worked through daily challenges. These are now amplified by several orders of magnitude. It's more important than ever that our companies learn to improve while becoming more efficient and resilient. But most previous efforts to transform business failed to sustain. We must learn from these earlier failures as we develop a new path forward.

In the 1980s, "they" told us Total Quality Management (TQM) would help us become more effective and efficient. The promised end-state was elusive, at best.

In the 1990s, "they" advised us that Business Process Improvement and then Re-engineering would make things better. And again, the results often fell far short of the promised end-state.

Currently, Lean and Six Sigma dominate as the next solution promising improved results. But without an integrated strategy, these too will fail to achieve and sustain our desired end-state.

Most readers are familiar with Lean and Six Sigma. But it's worth remembering these concepts are fairly fresh in our business world. Quite a few years earlier, there was Shewhart's Quality Statistical Control. And many years before that, we had Taylor's Scientific Management theory. In between, there have been other fads, but Lean and Six Sigma, or even Lean Six Sigma, are the current dominant focus.

A common theme has kept each of these approaches from reaching their full potential. As implemented, they each focus on the process without emphasizing the people or the culture. We may realize a temporary improvement, but this new state fails to sustain as the new and improved "way things get done around here." And there's a reason. Well, there are two reasons.

For the first reason, we'll need to wait until Chapter 4 to fully discuss why senior leaders haven't embraced Lean and Six Sigma in larger companies. Bob Emiliani's book, *The Triumph of Classical Management Over Lean Management*, provides an excellent read on this subject. While I don't want to diverge to the causes here, Emiliani provides keen insight that is worth a momentary pause:

> For the last 30 years, our eyes have told us this truth: There is a strong consensus of opinion among CEOs that if any of Lean is to be adopted, it is solely its tools. CEOs have expressed little interest in adopting Lean as a comprehensive system of management to replace classical Management. Much of it has to do with a failure to understand the thinking and interests of CEOs – particularly of large publicly traded corporations, who have long been the main target of interest for Lean transformation.

The reasons that American executives have resisted Lean have been elusive and poorly understood. While I agree with Professor Emiliani's conclusion above, I don't subscribe to any idea that success is only possible through an all-or-nothing approach. Later in this book, I'll introduce the Competing Values Framework. I'll show how the framework can help us find solutions that consider the best answer at a particular time. This includes using Lean in a support role for business transformation efforts.

Ken Blanchard helps us understand the second reason these methodologies haven't reached their full potential. Blanchard advises that leadership isn't something we do *to* people; leadership is something we do *with* people. An organization doesn't *implement* Operational Excellence as a methodology, model, or tool. An organization *realizes* Operational Excellence by integrating effective leadership, teamwork, problem-solving, systems thinking, and continuous improvement.

Each of these legacy continuous improvement methodologies attempted to change something with the way things get done. The important word here is *change*.

Those involved with organizational change understand one of the biggest hurdles to overcome is convincing people of the need to change in the first place. Our legacy improvement methodologies assume people have already bought-in and understand the connection between their behavior and desired improvement. Reality hijacked that idea long ago.

These methodologies can drive improvements. But successful results are usually tactical and tied to specific tasks. They plateau short of transformational solutions. Expanding these to strategically impact business execution systems, often believed to be beyond expectations, is in fact possible.

The term Lean, first coined by John Krafcik in a 1988 MIT management thesis, traces its roots to the Toyota Production System (TPS). The philosophy seeks to improve the flow of activities and reduce the cost of a process by reducing waste. With its beginnings in manufacturing, Lean relies upon a variety of statistical and quality control techniques to deliver improved results. The discipline originated under Eastern philosophies, and as we'll explore later, these can be quite different from Western philosophies.

Lean accomplishments in Japan don't mirror their achievement in America. The level of buy-in from senior leadership highlights these differences. Lean approaches process redesign at two levels. At the tactical or process level, *process kaizen* focuses on elimination of waste. At the enterprise level, *flow kaizen* focuses on improvements to high-level value streams. And as we can infer from Professor Emiliani's earlier words, flow kaizen is a rarity in American business.

Lean is a way of thinking that focuses on waste reduction. Six Sigma is a collection of tools and applications to reduce variation. While the intent of each methodology is good, we often depart from their intent to the point that we can sometimes struggle to see the forest through the trees.

I've often observed and participated with Lean Six Sigma experts removing waste and variation from a process. And these were often successful. But if the approach doesn't properly address the people equation, the improvements will always be fleeting. And here, the people equation includes the people completing the work and the senior leaders running the company.

In an extreme example, I've witnessed Lean methods used to remove minutes from manufacturing processes. The results were touted as an organizational achievement. But the practitioners lacked awareness to realize the employees responsible for the process were completely disengaged. A process improvement measured in minutes was negated by employee disengagement measured in hours.

I recently watched with more than passing interest a social media discourse between two Lean experts. Someone posted an article about Boeing's inability to manage complexity leading to the massive failure for their 737

Max aircraft. The article's assumptions about root cause resulted in significant disagreement. But far more interesting was the discourse between these two gentlemen and the different nuances in their approach to Lean.

Each man is a recognized authority in Lean. But they were talking past each other in ways I can't begin to describe. Each made an argument using unique Lean terms and qualifiers that the other wasn't familiar with, almost as if it was an intentional attempt to confuse. But it wasn't, and that's the point. Each of these men is a Lean expert, but they couldn't effectively communicate with one another because each was trying to "out-Lean" the other to prove their point.

Lean uses terms like kanban, gemba, muda, mura, and muri. Some then add additional qualifiers, such as gemba 1, gemba 2, and gemba 3. Over-reliance upon these foreign terms only serves to keep the philosophy from being more widely understood and applied. And by *foreign*, I'm not referring to the Japanese language, but something "strange or unfamiliar." Lean purists will not agree with the preceding argument. But that doesn't change its truth.

I often found myself questioning the fever behind these new strategies, introduced early in my career. I suspected they weren't much more than normalizers for standard practices. I watched and even obtained my own certifications. But I never believed these methodologies would be the primary tool to drive transformational improvement.

Over the latter part of my career, I've worked with some gifted people that unconditionally qualify as experts in Lean and Six Sigma. I would classify few as masters. And the difference is significant.

Mastery is the ability to reduce incredible complexity to profound simplicity.

An expert mathematician may be gifted at solving complex mathematical problems, but unable to explain his methods so that others achieve similar results. In this context, experts sometimes fail to provide the complete solution. A master mathematician's skills go beyond the numbers and equations. A master conveys the subject in a manner that students quickly understand the application and how to use it for their own benefit.

A company may have experts in continuous improvement, but that doesn't mean they'll be successful sustaining strategic improvements. The reason ties back to why experts don't provide the total solution.

Masters are rare, very rare. Using legacy continuous improvement tools, mastery improves the likelihood that improvements sustain as the way things get done. But because few of our initiatives are led by masters, results are normally fleeting.

But when approaching the situation through the lens of Operational Excellence, the system expands. The problem now includes assessing the values and beliefs, the culture and marketspace, the systems and structures, and the leadership and strategy. We have framed the problem much differently. While it would be nice to have a master, this approach allows an expert to deliver sustained results.

We all recognize that we must start to do things differently. Lean and Six Sigma will be great tools for us to use as we move forward. But we will need more than just these tools.

Many Lean Six Sigma practitioners and authors have begun to tout their philosophies as strategies to help companies recover from the coronavirus pandemic. On their own, they won't be enough. We will need more than tactical solutions. We will need to change our tactical solutions and our strategic thinking to employ strategies that work together for a holistic benefit. We will need to frame the problem through the lens of Operational Excellence.

WHAT OPERATIONAL EXCELLENCE LOOKS LIKE

Companies may set out to implement a plan to obtain an ISO certification or to implement Lean, Six Sigma, or other improvement plans. But they don't set out to *implement* Operational Excellence. Or at least they won't do so successfully. Rather, companies *realize* Operational Excellence over time once they've successfully integrated strategies, business processes, and the people towards a common goal.

Such a company, an operationally excellent company, will have lower operational risk, optimized operating costs, more engaged employees, higher revenues, and more delighted customers than its competitors. It will also be more resilient. The following characteristics would be commonplace for the way things get done within a company that has reached this level of performance.

Values and Beliefs

the company's beliefs are documented · values are clear, concise, and understood · employee and company values align · people value and respect one another · leaders focus on changing what people think rather than how they act · people desire to move beyond average · people believe they can do *both* this *and* that · people are uncomfortable with mediocrity · employees openly share bad news as quickly as good news · the company's *why* is known and understood by the employees and the customers

Culture

risk-thinking is part of normal thought · younger generations with new beliefs are welcomed into the culture · emotional thought stimulates effective working relations · steady compliance is regularly rewarded · the culture embraces integrity and accountability · diversity of thought, ideas, and backgrounds are valued · lessons from the past are learned to affect the future · difficult decisions are made without hesitation · change planning involves those affected by the change · conflict is healthy and effectively managed · problem-solving is a habit · time is taken to celebrate wins · time spent in meetings is optimized · friction is minimized · the relentless pursuit of continual improvement is how things get done

Leadership and Strategy

top leadership is committed to excellence · strategic goals link to tactical execution · leadership is humble and maintains respect for the individual · effective planning drives execution · leadership styles align with business needs · values-based leadership is the dominant leadership style · goals are based on outcomes rather than activities · leaders provide safe environments · individual goals tie to the company strategy · objectives seek breakthrough performance · risks and opportunities are managed with equal vigor · communication is continuous and effective · strategic goals align the company to one vision

Systems and Structures

processes align and integrate with the systems · the organizational structure supports current business needs · the enterprise structure is collaborative and responsive · agility dominates over bureaucracy · analysis, synthesis, and systems thinking help solve problems · intentional steps are taken to avoid and eliminate sub-optimization · different management systems are complementary and align under a consolidated business management system · the business management system is integrated as part of the business planning cycle · internal systems and structures are designed to be resilient

Marketspace

innovation serves as a competitive advantage · leadership styles align with the current organizational life cycle · breakthrough goals help expand into new markets · the company employs ethical actions to grow · investment expenses focus on future growth · the company understands its place in the marketspace and the context of the organization · organizational learning provides a competitive advantage · sustained profits are maximized—costs are optimized · costs are viewed as an opportunity to make reductions and return value to the customer

People

employees are collaborative, empowered, and engaged · roles and responsibilities are defined and understood · teamwork is effective and leverages greater returns · management is aligned across all layers and business units · victimhood is not tolerated · people are intentional · the workplace does not exclude emotions · people are afforded the structure to thrive outside of teams · the organizational construct has adapted to changing work environments · multi-generations work together and leverage each other's strengths · management recognize the people as best-in-class

Processes

the company's core processes are defined · the enterprise architecture and process architecture align with the business model · processes are streamlined to eliminate bureaucracy · processes detect errors early in the value stream · analysts are empowered to provide data that drives decisions·procedures are written as clear guidelines·process owners and governance are clear·audits ensure process accountability·effective problem-solving provides a competitive advantage·administrative approvals are efficient and streamlined·the costs of quality are understood and optimized·users recognize the processes as best-in-class

Products

product designs empathize with customer needs·the people making the products believe in the products·quality is uncompromised and assured at the source·the product design adds value to the customer·innovation and creativity are valued and rewarded·quality is designed into the product·the design concept represents how the product works vice how it looks·the organization tolerates fast failures and provides safe environments to innovate·customers recognize the products as best-in-class

Customer Experience

core processes are based on value streams originating from the customer·the business has close and personal empathy for its customers·change that doesn't add value to the customer is rejected·the entire organization is mission and customer focused·seeking a delighted customer is more important than a satisfied customer·customers are actively cultivated as advocates·balance is maintained between focusing inward and outward·everyone understands the purpose of the business is to create value for the customer·the business is resilient and able to provide products and services when needed most

Achieving a workplace defined by these characteristics is difficult. It may take years to achieve such a state. But we must start somewhere. A thousand-mile walk begins with the first step. I'll discuss ideas needed to stimulate thoughts to achieve this preferred state as we move through the book.

But before examining these closer, there are two important precursors to achieving this readiness level we're calling excellence. As we embark on this journey, how well we *communicate*, and how well we *lead change*, will each play a large part in how close we get to excellence.

COMMUNICATING OUR INTENT

George Bernard Shaw is rumored to have stated, "The single biggest problem in communication is the illusion that it has taken place." Research indicates communication shortfalls remain one of the more common reasons our transformation efforts struggle. The communication message associated with our strategy to achieve excellence must be clear and consistent. And it must be continually repeated.

It's been said we need to be exposed to new thoughts 151 times before we get it. The first 50 times, we don't hear it. The second 50 times, we don't understand it. The third 50 times, we don't believe it. But after hearing the message the 151st time, we get it. Deming would agree, as he informed us we cannot hear what we don't understand.

Effective communication facilitates openness and improves attitudes in this environment of change. It helps people become more open-minded and receptive to things that are new, mostly due to the process of reducing uncertainty.

Withholding information, either intentional or unintentional, creates a communication vacuum. The unintended consequences from ineffective communication result in employees providing their own answers. Those who are the most concerned fill this vacuum with gossip, rumors, and misinformation.

Studies reveal the reason many communication strategies struggle is that they tend to be one way. They focus on providing information with little intent to receive information back.

The other side of communication is listening. Receiving is just as important as transmitting.

For communication to be effective, it must be received, understood, and provide useful information to help those affected. One-way communication may be appropriate during the initial stages of change when people have high commitment and little competence. But as people become familiar with the change and their competence increases, communication must start to go both ways.

The employees' concerns must be heard and acknowledged. Failure to do so will inhibit trust. We lead them through the unknown by providing direction. But we also need to listen to ensure we're building a foundation for trust.

Effective listening requires a deep commitment to hearing and understanding others' concerns. For the leader, it requires that they also hear their own inner voice and pause to reflect on its message.

Communication involves a social exchange between giver and receiver. This exchange helps engender trust in the change initiative. We'll need this trust. Without it, we'll never gain commitment and won't be able to lead our company towards excellence.

LEADING THE MOVEMENT TO EXCELLENCE

Before any company considers a serious commitment to excellence, it must first have an effective system in place for organizational change management (OCM).

Volumes of books have been written on change management—some of these are fine works. Many companies hire specialists and create OCM departments. Other companies choose to bring in consultants. While this is a fair approach, it's better to teach our people to fish. My previous work on the subject emphasizes middle managers as the key to effectively leading change from *within* our organizations.

I won't detract from this book's purpose and go too far down this change management road. But once top management makes the commitment to pursue excellence, transformational change *will* ensue. This will be *planned* change. We'll be creating what doesn't yet exist. We must be prepared.

There are two primary sources for this planned change: *needs* and *ideas*. As we'll see later, these needs and ideas are common drivers for many new things in our companies.

Change driven from needs is often associated with perceived problems or opportunities. It results from forcing functions in the external environment that we can't ignore. It's typically driven from the customer, competition, or regulation. Needs-driven change tends to be top-down and often originates from executive management.

Change driven from ideas, on the other hand, is often associated with creativity and innovation. This change comes from forcing functions in the external environment that are less mandatory than needs, although just as critical. It's typically derived from suppliers, trade movements, and research. Ideas-driven change tends to be bottom-up and typically originates from within the organization.

Kurt Lewin is the father of *planned* change. Lewin's model defines the process to move a measured characteristic from an initial undesired state to a final desired state. The model emphasizes the need to discard old behaviors, structures, and processes before adopting new behaviors, structures, and processes. The heart of Lewin's approach is the three-step process of *unfreeze, move,* and *freeze.*

The first step, *unfreeze,* focuses on getting people to disconfirm what they believe to be true for how things are accomplished. This initial phase is concerned with directly affecting peoples' readiness and motivation to change. The second step is the action to *move* from this initial state, perceived to be unsatisfactory, to the new desired state. The last step, *freeze,* is the process of making these new behaviors the new way things get done, to make them a habit.

Lewin also developed a construct to help us understand how the forces of change work against one another. Lewin's *force field analysis* of Figure 1.1

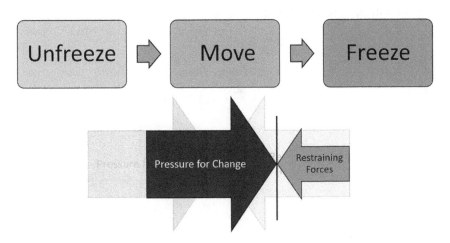

FIGURE 1.1

Lewin change and force field model.

describes the relative strengths of the driving and restraining forces working for and against change.

Driving forces move the organization towards change while restraining forces push back. The driving forces *activate* the restraining forces and cause them to come about. The natural tendency to move meets an equal resistance that fights the movement. The change emerging is the product of interaction of these opposing forces. We facilitate change acceptance by decreasing the restraining forces through participative involvement, communication, and training.

Change will struggle to achieve measurable benefits and become the new way things get done if the forces resisting it are stronger than the forces driving it. Simply applying a larger driving force won't work. Any increase to the driving forces is countered by restraining forces of equal magnitude.

To reach the desired state, we <u>must</u> reduce the restraining forces. The best way to do this is to involve people in the change. Put some of them on the change leadership team. Involve them in the pilot. Communicate to them. Then communicate to them more. And then still more after that. Provide them value-added training but only after they've been exposed to the newness of the change. Allow them, the people effected by the change, to be involved in shaping the change.

If we do this, we'll be ahead of this change thing. And that will serve us well on our path to excellence.

Part II

Things We Don't See

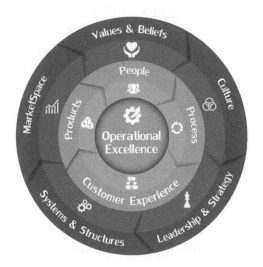

Think about the last time you were audited by an external activity. Did the auditor find obvious errors that you overlooked? If so, you're not alone. It happens far more often than you may think.

The reason external auditors find these exceptions has nothing to do with them. It has everything to do with us. We simply fail to notice them.

The fact that we fail to notice things has been subject to interesting studies. They even have a name for it—perceptual blindness. The studies argue stimuli overcome us to the point that we limit our focus and therefore fail to see the obvious.

One of the more entertaining experiments here is *The Invisible Gorilla*, made famous by the video and then book by Christopher Chabris and Daniel Simons. Count me within the group that initially failed to notice their gorilla.

Research into this area focuses on how we use our brains. I'm not qualified for such assessments, but there may be another reason we don't notice things. I believe we're conditioned *not* to notice them. We see things that are wrong, but we don't *notice* them.

Our education system teaches us to disregard our perceptions. We're taught that examining our thoughts and perceptions is unimportant. We're conditioned to document our research by citing another author's work instead of exploring our own thoughts, feelings, and ideas. This results in a conditioned mindset that what we think is somehow less important than what others more famous have thought.

Over time, we eventually struggle to notice ourselves.

We need new thoughts to believe that what we notice matters. What we notice is important. We notice things *because* they are important.

We can take some time to notice things around us right now. This means using all of our senses. I'll bet we become aware of something we previously didn't notice. Do this simple thing frequently, just a couple of times each day, and suddenly the world around us starts to look different.

Noticing things, and then thinking closely about what we notice, may result in looking at our company through a different lens. The result of our observations will be helpful on our journey to excellence.

2

Validating Our Values and Beliefs

Average is a learned behavior. We tend to seek comfort in a shared mediocrity. But we're looking to rise beyond average. We're looking to reject this comfort with mediocrity. We're looking for excellence.

To do this, we need to unlearn some things. Lewin referred to this unlearning as disconfirmation. He knew it to be the critical first step on the path to achieving organizational change.

We start this unlearning by shifting our thoughts to understand things at their core. And the root of that discussion within our companies, made up of people, is to understand the values and beliefs that form our thoughts of what is real and what is not real.

WHAT WE BELIEVE AND VALUE

People act the way they do because they have beliefs that cause them to think certain things and behave in certain ways. Because words are important, we need to pause here to ensure we have a common understanding of these "things" we're about to discuss.

Beliefs are basic principles, our presupposition of knowledge—something we innately understand to be true. They are foundational. An average adult has hundreds of thousands of beliefs within their total belief system. This system includes inconsequential, derived, authority, and core beliefs. Our belief system forms the mental models that drive our behavior within the surrounding culture.

Achieving excellence requires change. When people talk about organizational change, those good at it advise there are some foundational truths—things we should do to increase the likelihood of success. The first of these is that when we seek to affect change, we don't try to change the way people act. Instead, we want to change the way they think. And we do this by addressing their beliefs, what they innately understand to be true.

Not all beliefs have the same strength of conviction; but not all beliefs must change when seeking cultural change. Efforts here focus on inconsequential and derived beliefs. This is good news for us. Changing core beliefs is almost impossible and beyond the ethical dimensions of what we're discussing.

Beliefs form the foundation of an organization's culture. Moving towards excellence requires changes to the culture, so we begin our journey by affecting changes within this belief system. The next chapter dives deeper into culture. For now, we're concentrating on beliefs that make up the culture. But to be honest, grasping these concepts can be difficult.

One of the problems we face with understanding culture is the lack of any tangible substance that we can view and dissect. Culture and the beliefs that form its make up are abstracts. We can't see them, although we *can* see their residual effects.

A play on the oft-used iceberg analogy helps us visualize beliefs and their importance in this realm.

Imagine an iceberg represents a company's culture. Below the waterline at the base of the iceberg, deep within the informal organization, exist the undefined *experiences* that occur throughout the workday.

These are the "things" that happen to us, that we observe in others, and that we make happen, every day.

Our *experiences* form perceptions that become ingrained within us. These different *experiences* form together to become our *beliefs*.

The formal and informal organizations both generate beliefs. Those below the waterline are the "underlying assumptions," the unconscious beliefs and perceptions that drive behavior. Beliefs above the waterline are the "espoused beliefs" as formally stated by the organization.

These *beliefs* drive our *actions*. And the collective *actions* work together to produce *results*.

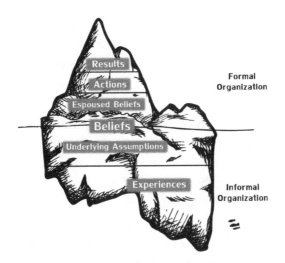

FIGURE 2.1

Beliefs within the culture.

There's more happening here than the simple image of Figure 2.1 can depict. And that's because beliefs often conceal their true importance to a company's success.

Remember, we're looking to move beyond average. To do this, we need people to behave differently. And to do this, we need them to start and think differently. But they won't think differently if we ask them to do something they don't believe or don't value.

Values and beliefs are different things. Beliefs are pure and if measured, independent of any other measure. A value is the product of comparison against another concept. A value is like a metric. A metric by itself doesn't determine goodness; rather, a metric helps us measure performance compared against a known standard.

Having this context, a value is an enduring belief one phenomenon is preferred over another. Values by themselves don't determine good from bad but merely provide the standard to gauge comparison. As we remember from Philosophy 101, there are two types of values: ends and means. Ends values correlate to the future desired state. Means values align to the preferred path to bring about a specific end.

The collection of an individual's ends and means values creates their values point of view and comprises their value system. Our values point of view helps define how we see the world and establishes our behavior along the way. Over time, our social display of these behaviors forms our character. And as we've all recently observed, a crisis doesn't build character, but it does tend to reveal it.

Around the midpoint of my career, I joined a communications company to help turnaround a struggling division. This large company had an unusually loyal employee base. Average length of company service exceeded 20 years. These people didn't necessarily embrace change. And that's exactly what I was asked to bring.

During my introduction to the division, I spent considerable time discussing my values. I closed my talk by acknowledging that I didn't expect them to believe my words. I did expect them to observe my behavior and make their own assessments whether my actions supported my stated values.

The team I was about to lead was well rooted in its culture and didn't particularly welcome an outsider. Two years into my tenure, the leader of the informal organization approached me to discuss this initial meeting. He stated they were closely watching me. I already knew this to be the case.

Then he surprised me. He indirectly admitted to initially working against me behind the scenes. But then acknowledged that as he watched our progress, he began to buy-in to our new direction. He then confessed that I brought much needed change and had earned their trust through my approach. He told me they had learned to believe me.

I was able to positively influence the group and the informal leader's beliefs. Changing a culture to pursue operational excellence requires these types of changes to the belief system.

Just like individuals, an organization has a value system but from the collective perspective. To move towards excellence, we must be aware of these value systems. A company's value system evolves over time. It takes a while for different *experiences* to form collective *beliefs* that people see driving *actions* and *results* to compare preferred behavior to value.

Different events can shake up this value system. A new leader, new ownership, or new marketspace can each impact a company's value system. We've just experienced a pandemic that will forever change our core beliefs and our value systems. Even before this catastrophic event, significant shake-ups were already creating momentous change to our employee demographics. And these demographic changes have been driving major shifts to our value systems.

Millennials, who some of us once feared with veiled malice, now make up the largest demographic of our companies. They think different. And they value different things. Different events shaped their younger years than those experienced by Gen X and Baby Boomers. These different events provided them different experiences. Their different experiences caused them to form different beliefs. With these different beliefs, they often value different things than those who came before them.

We maybe could have previously ignored what they believed to be important. But no more. Those of us who aren't Millennials must start to understand their beliefs and respect their values. These men and women represent our leadership future for the next 30 years. If we want to move towards excellence, we must find a common ground with this important group of people.

We also mustn't discount Gen Z, who have beliefs different even from Millennials, and will be here soon. These young people will be changing how we define work. That's just one of the many significant changes they'll be bringing. And with these changes will come new emotions.

Change associated with pursuing excellence is an affective event, meaning that it's emotion laden. Emotions *are* present, despite the best attempts by some companies to keep them out.

Those pursuing excellence must recognize people exposed to change develop strong emotions about what's happening. We can facilitate an emotional connection through a common value system—a value system composed of beliefs. Those things we believe to be true.

To be successful in our pursuit of excellence, we must connect with people on a personal level—an emotional level—to help gain their commitment. To do this, we must be aware of the different value systems in play.

A weak correlation between a company and employee value systems creates problems. A lack of congruence here impedes change. The resulting product is change initiatives that fail to achieve their intended objectives and, therefore, will cause us to arrive at something short of excellence.

DOCUMENTING WHAT WE BELIEVE

My wife and I relocate often. Each move results in the need to find a new church. When moving to a new community, we preview church websites to help identify choices. We prefer Baptist services. While most Baptist churches have similar values, their beliefs can vary dramatically.

Many churches openly profess their values and even advertise them on their websites. While we are interested in a church's values, our main concerns are their beliefs. We want to make sure we're joining a group that holds similar ideas to what we believe. Joining a church that we don't share similar beliefs with would quickly result in dissatisfaction, discomfort, confusion, and regret.

The same disconnect happens if any of us join a company where we have disconnected beliefs. Or if we stayed the same but somehow the company's belief system changed.

Most companies create mission statements to help identify their purpose and why they exist. Many also create vision statements to motivate and inspire their employees toward what they hope to become. Some go even further and state their values to help guide behavior.

The mission, vision, and values each complement one another and describe what the company is and what it seeks to be. But even detailed descriptors here only tell a partial story. We get the whole story through beliefs—the presuppositions about why the organization is what it is.

As Simon Sinek has helped many of us better understand, it's important to understand *why* a company does what it does. The *why* that Sinek speaks and writes about directly correlates to the company's beliefs. A company that doesn't understand its *why* will never achieve excellence.

Remember, beliefs often conceal their true importance to a company's success. A beliefs statement is the same thing as the company's *why*. It's what the company believes. When we seek to change a culture to move towards excellence, we must change the way people think. But we cannot change what they think if we're not aware of what they believe.

Beliefs are too important to the company's success to keep them secret. We therefore <u>must</u> document them with a formal beliefs statement.

Often beliefs statements are combined with the values statement. That's a fine approach, as long as they *are* documented.

Creating a beliefs statement is important. It's especially important, but few companies do so. It documents what the people and the organization believe. Mission, vision, and value statements are crucial. But they're still not as important as documenting what we believe in—what we believe to be true.

Recall Lewin's basic process to facilitate change is to unfreeze, move, and freeze. We want to unfreeze, or disconfirm, what people believe to be true for how things get accomplished. We do this by providing opportunities for different experiences that demonstrate there is a better way for things to get done. Over time, these new experiences drive new beliefs which drive new actions and *will* deliver improved results.

These ideas are possibly more important now than ever before. This is a time of disruption. Beliefs form the foundation of a company's culture. Strong cultures may be able to handle this disruption. Weaker cultures will struggle to do so. Our companies must have a clear purpose for why they exist, along with a strong set of understood and documented beliefs and core values. Such a state is the foundation for any company seeking to become more resilient and operationally excellent.

MEASURING WHAT WE VALUE

Different values drive different behaviors. I wanted to know why.

I was curious why different people seeking the same result pursue it through methods that sometimes seem to compete against one another. I knew the way people think drives their behavior and how they think is dependent upon their values and beliefs.

I also knew that we don't always value the same behavior. So that's where I started my search. I researched the interaction of these sometimes-opposing values. My research quickly led to the Competing Values Framework (CVF).

Originally put forth by Robert Quinn and John Rohrbaugh in 1983, the CVF developed out of research to determine indicators of organizational effectiveness. Others have since expanded the original work to produce a framework of theories that assume paradoxes are not only present but are in fact required for effective management.

The CVF is a simple sense-making model that serves as a learning system. The framework helps identify "guidelines that can enable leaders to diagnose and manage the interrelationships, congruencies, and contradictions" across an organization. It offers a simple model that helps us make sense of things through seeing organizational life with more clarity.

Applying the CVF requires us to shift our thought processes. We typically approach choices with a mindset that we must select either one choice or another. The framework helps us understand we don't have to accept a forced choice that isn't required.

Instead, the framework assumes we approach choices as one option *and* the other but from varying degrees of temporal emphasis. This allows us to transition from choosing between good and bad to between good and good. The actual framework has many variants. The base structure is a simple quad model based on a set of two dimensions that represent different tensions or "competing values" present in our companies.

The first dimension represents the *focus of the organization*, plotted on the x-axis along the spectrum from an internal focus on integration to an external focus on differentiation. The second dimension along the y-axis represents the *focus of preference for structure*, contrasted along the spectrum from stability and control to flexibility and change. The two dimensions form the quadrants of opposing values as indicated in Figure 2.2.

The model's framework provides four core dimensions that can represent a variety of concepts, from evaluating organizations to creating customer value. The underlying idea is that any one dimension is the dominant trait at any one time. But it is not the only choice.

A quadrant can represent the dominant style of a person, a functional team, or an entire company. The key to unlocking the framework is to appreciate the parameters don't represent an all or nothing approach. People and organizations can, and do, compete with their opposing quadrant and engage in trade-offs to obtain desired outcomes.

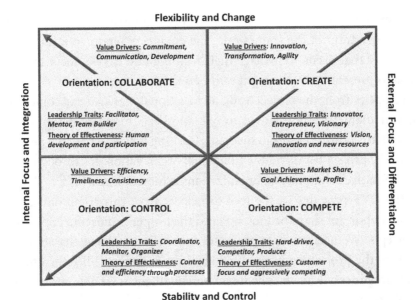

FIGURE 2.2

The Competing Values Framework. (Adapted with permission from *Diagnosing and Changing Organizational Culture.*)

While neither organizations nor individuals can be equally strong in all four quadrants at any moment, the model suggests leaders and organizations maintain a balance between the four to be most effective. Tensions are designed-in to our organizations. These paradoxes are realities, but they don't equate to all or nothing. We err if we interpret these choices as such. We can have both, just not at the same time.

To illustrate an application, let's examine the typical matrix structure. Under a matrix construct, functions are responsible for staffing, training, and developing employees while project teams are responsible for product realization. Tensions often exist between the functional organizations and the project teams. At times, the two groups can appear diametrically opposed. Success, and excellence, resides in the ability to find trade-offs so that both can achieve their goals.

Imagine this matrix structure as an R&D project team composed of engineers. The project team needs the engineers to be innovative, agile, and exhibit behavioral characteristics present mostly in the upper right *create* quadrant of the framework. The engineers report to a functional manager that needs to manage their training and development through tenants present in the lower left *control* quadrant.

Priorities from the project lead and functional manager can sometimes appear diametrically opposed to one another. This is by design of the matrix structure. The key to success is learning how to satisfy the needs of both the project team and the functional organization. It's through those collaborative solutions that organizations achieve a win-win.

The CVF provides us the tool to help achieve this compromise. But more important than the tool, we need the proper mindset to apply these concepts. We need thought processes that help us achieve the objectives of *both* the project team *and* functional management. I'll return to this thought process, known as *both/and thinking*, later as we dive into a deeper application.

I'll employ the CVF often as the book progresses. I'll do so each time there are choices between competing interests. The framework helps us find solutions that are choices between good and good. And it has practical applications that will help us on our journey to excellence.

3

Honing Our Culture

Subscribers to chaos theory advise that we live in a complex world of randomness and uncertainty—a world characterized by surprise, rapid change, and confusion. Considering the world events that we've recently experienced, I now agree.

Our world is changing faster than many of us can keep up. Our job as leaders and managers is to try to measure, control, and predict this unfolding drama.

To positively affect this chaos, we must focus our attention on the culture. The famous quote that *culture eats strategy for breakfast* is understated. I wish I had a more elegant way to say it, but I don't. Yet sometimes things don't need improved upon. And I do know that when pursuing excellence in our new environment as it's being defined before us, there will be nothing more important to success than understanding the company's culture.

THE WAY THINGS GET DONE AROUND HERE

Culture is a complex thing. A complex thing that can be difficult to understand. But we must have more than a basic understanding of our culture to be successful in the pursuit of excellence. We'll leave formal culture analysis to the experts. But something I've learned along my journey is that to be able to lead successfully, we *must* understand the surrounding culture and its associated interdependencies.

For example, if we're attempting to affect a change to reporting relationships within the formal organization, we *must* consider the hidden residual effects on the informal organization. Failure to do so often results in unintended consequences.

This book focuses on the actions needed to move from average to excellent performance. It's not a book on organizational culture. There are many good books on that subject. From a technical standpoint, one of my favorites is Schein's *Organizational Culture and Leadership*. For practical applications, I prefer Cameron and Quinn's *Diagnosing and Changing Organizational Culture*. Rather than attempt a detailed analysis here, our discussion will focus on those specific cultural elements, either their presence or absence, that we must hone or mitigate to move closer to excellence.

Just to make sure we're thinking the same thing as we discuss culture, let's review how it's defined. Within *Organizational Culture and Leadership*, Schein formally defines culture as follows:

> The accumulated shared learning of that group as it solves its problems of external adaptation and internal integration; which has worked well enough to be considered valid and, therefore, to be taught to new members as the correct way to perceive, think, feel, and behave in relation to those problems. This accumulated learning is a pattern or system of beliefs, values, and behavioral norms that come to be taken for granted as basic assumptions and eventually drop out of awareness.

That's a descriptive definition which helps us understand. But we can less formally define culture as the values, ways of thinking, managerial styles, paradigms, and approaches to problem-solving and decision-making that are used to get things done. And we can reduce this even more simply to "the way things get done around here." I prefer this simpler definition.

People are often not aware of the culture until it is challenged. Pursuing excellence will require us to challenge the culture continuously. Goodness will come from this increased awareness.

Earlier I stated culture was an abstract, that we can't see it. But there's a tool we can use to provide a relational image to "view" the culture. It can help us become more aware of how things are now versus how we desire them to be in a future state, an excellent state.

The Competing Values Framework (CVF), introduced in Chapter 2, provides us a vehicle to better understand the culture. The four different culture types identified in Figure 3.1 form the foundation of the framework.

The Organizational Culture Assessment Instrument (OCAI), based on the CVF, provides a visual as a plot of the relative strength of each distinct culture type. The instrument evaluates the culture across six characteristics to plot a graphic representation of the overall organizational culture.

The value of the OCAI comes from comparing the present culture to the future, preferred culture. The people making up the organization define the characteristics for this preferred culture. The OCAI presents a series of questions and provides a tool to visualize the comparison of our answers.

In the representative example of Figure 3.2, respondents indicated the current culture to be equally balanced between the *Adhocracy*, *Clan*, and *Hierarchy* elements but with a dominant focus on the *Market* culture. The respondents believed the best interest of the company would be served by keeping a moderated focus on *Adhocracy* and *Hierarchy*. But they sought to shift primary focus from a *Market* to a *Clan*-oriented culture. Cameron and Quinn's *Diagnosing and Changing Organizational Culture* provides specific action plans we can use to affect this shift.

The OCAI provides a valuable tool to compare the current culture to the preferred culture needed to achieve excellence. The theory behind the CVF provides specific actions we can implement to close the gap between the two cultural states—current and desired.

I've administered the OCAI many times. Most times it provided value on the journey to excellence. But a few times, it didn't. There's a common reason some efforts weren't successful. It ties back to lack of buy-in from senior leadership. While senior leaders tolerated the assessments, they didn't accept the idea we could help shape the culture by identifying desired characteristics for a future state.

The Clan Culture	The Adhocracy Culture
A very friendly place to work where people share a lot of themselves. It is like an extended family. The leaders, or head of the organization, are considered to be mentors and, maybe even, parent figures. The organization is held together by loyalty or tradition. Commitment is high. The organization emphasizes the long-term benefit of human resource development and attaches great importance to cohesion and morale. Success is defined in terms of sensitivity to customers and concern for people. The organization places a premium on teamwork, participation, and consensus.	A dynamic, entrepreneurial, and creative place to work. People stick their necks out and take risks. The leaders are considered to be innovators and risk takers. The glue that holds the organization together is commitment to experimentation and innovation. The emphasis is on being on the leading edge. The organization's long-term emphasis is on growth and acquiring new resources. Success means gaining unique and new products or services. Being a product or service leader is important. The organization encourages individual initiative and freedom.
The Hierarchy Culture	The Market Culture
A very formalized and structured place to work. Procedures govern what people do. The leaders pride themselves on being good coordinators and organizers, who are efficiency-minded. Maintaining a smoothly running organization is most critical. Formal rules and policies hold the organization together. The long-term concern is on stability and performance with efficient, smooth operations. Success is defined in terms of dependable delivery, smooth scheduling, and low cost. The management of employees is concerned with secure employment and predictability.	A results-oriented organization. The major concern is getting the job done. People are competitive and goal oriented. The leaders are hard drivers, producers, and competitors. They are tough and demanding. The glue that holds the organization together is an emphasis on winning. Reputations and success are common concerns. The long-term focus is on competitive actions and achievement of measurable goals and targets. Success is defined in terms of market share and penetration. Competitive pricing and market leadership are important. The organizational style is hard-driving competitiveness.

FIGURE 3.1

CVF culture types. (Adapted with permission from *Diagnosing and Changing Organizational Culture.*)

We must accept that not every attempt at transformation will be successful. Some companies will choose to remain committed to average performance.

LEARNING

Our approach to learning helps define our culture—it may be more important than many of us realize. Peter Senge tells us the speed at which an organization learns is its only true sustainable competitive advantage. I believe the effectiveness at which we solve problems is another sustainable

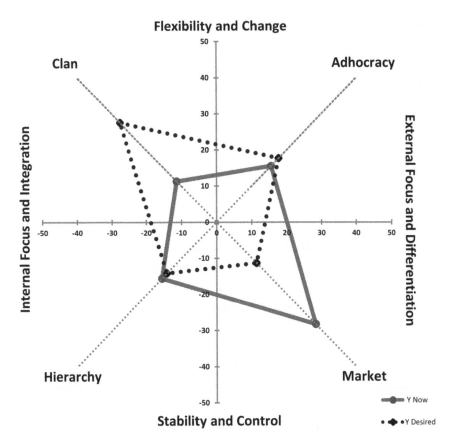

FIGURE 3.2

Culture represented by the OCAI. (Adapted with permission from *Diagnosing and Changing Organizational Culture*.)

competitive advantage. Yet one could easily argue problem-solving is in fact learning.

Learning from the past is an advanced leadership skill. Foresight is a characteristic that enables a leader to understand these lessons from the past, how they interact with the realities of the present, and then use them to make better decisions in the future.

A company becomes a learning organization when it generates new ways of thinking that are learned and shared with others to generate new behaviors.

Learning affects our underlying assumptions and beliefs which ultimately drive new behaviors. These new behaviors become the new "way things get done around here" and produce our sought-after improved results.

Think about some of the largest and most successful companies—let's consider Amazon, Apple, and Microsoft. I'm sure we would agree these companies each have effective systems in place to ensure they're continuously learning, adapting, and changing course.

But these companies are world class. Most aren't, by simple definition. And most of our companies struggle to make that leap to become a learning organization.

Organizational theorists have yet to agree on a common definition for what it means to be a learning organization. But we may be over-thinking this. To simplify things, let's consider the definition of learning as "knowledge or skill acquired by instruction or study." Having this modest definition, we can review four distinct levels of organizational learning:

- **Individual** – discrete learning of new ideas or skills by individuals
- **Group** – knowledge shared from one individual of a group to others within the group
- **Organizational** – structured learning across an organization
- **Inter-organizational** – sharing knowledge between allied entities to learn from one another

I've seen learning systems record pages of parameters associated with a potential learning event. The parameters often include dozens of attributes and classifications to document intended lessons. Simply recording attributes of an event does nothing to facilitate learning. A database of lessons doesn't help us learn from what happened and, more importantly, achieve improved results at the next opportunity.

As an alternative, I propose that organizations start to learn the same way that people learn. We learn through repetition and exposure.

People progress through defined stages as they gain competence in a specific task. Situational leadership theory recognizes this learning pattern with its four development levels. A more detailed theory from psychology, introduced in the same year as situational leadership theory by Martin Broadwell, relates people learn by progressing through four stages of competence.

In the first stage, *unconscious incompetence*, the learner has no knowledge or awareness of the skill. By the second stage, *conscious incompetence*, the learner has become aware of the skill. This represents the onset of learning. In the third stage, *conscious competence*, the learner begins to apply the skill but must practice and concentrate to achieve desired results. And by the final stage, *unconscious competence*, the learner has expertise and familiarity so the skill can be completed unconsciously.

Considering these stages of competence, the most we can hope to achieve through reviewing lessons or participating in a classroom training is to move from unconscious incompetence to conscious incompetence. But this is only the onset of learning. We want to get to unconscious competence. And we do this through increased exposure and repetition.

The same reason lessons learned systems fail to instill learning haunts the success for most of our internal training efforts. We provide great training packages, and then abandon our employees.

A better approach, and one that facilitates improved learning, is to develop sustainment efforts that provide reinforcement training. Under this approach, a lesson management system should provide triggers that re-introduce the lesson at periodic times after initial review. Through this increased exposure, the people, their function, and even the company can progress towards unconscious competence. They can "learn" information determined to be important enough to record as a lesson.

We're all familiar with these systems companies implement to help employees learn. But we also need to reconsider a system that helps companies learn from the employees.

Employee suggestion programs have been hit and miss, but mostly miss, within our companies. It's an understatement to say effective use of such programs has been random. They often start with a bang and with great intent, but we seldom follow through and use them to help move towards excellence. These are indeed learning systems, as we must always remember, no one of us is as smart as all of us.

Without an intentional plan and engaged management, all suggestion programs eventually fail. We tend to view these as short-term solutions to current problems. We need to change this mindset. Suggestion programs often require a going-in commitment of a three- to five-year timeline.

For the initial phase, management's most important task is to encourage voluntary suggestions. Initially, these may not be very good, and that's okay. It's more important for employees to experience management reviewing suggestions and acting. In the second phase, management should transition to helping employees create better suggestions that define the problem, causes, and suggested corrective actions. Then in the final phase, with momentum in place and buy-in from both management and employees, emphasis can shift to require that employees define the benefit of the suggestion.

Most of our suggestion programs start with the final phase. In our American results-oriented culture, we're often impatient and want immediate payback. Most cultural changes, to include employees buying into the value of a suggestion program, take several years to realize positive benefits. But the potential reward here is worth the investment and delayed payback.

We must often slow down to go fast when seeking to raise performance from average to excellent.

FRICTION

Friction is that which resists our forward progress. It's the product from lack of alignment, poor procedures, poorly designed systems, indecisiveness, and fear.

Friction continually works against our efforts to reach excellence. It can make simple tasks seem almost impossible. It costs us time and money—much more than many leaders realize. We must be intentional to identify friction and then remove it. While we'll never eliminate all friction from the culture, we can mitigate against its unfettered proliferation.

But sometimes, we focus on the wrong things.

Not taking intentional action to remove friction is one of those times. Roger Dooley advises in his book *Friction* that the cost to the US economy exceeds three trillion dollars a year. I would argue it's something that needs our attention.

I mentioned fear as a source of friction. That rates an explanation. Fear generates friction through two sources, each with a different origin. But both trace their root to leaders not qualified for their position.

Sometimes, those without the requisite leadership skills are promoted into higher positions. I wish it happened less frequently, but that's a different discussion. A weak leader with control over resources tends to base decisions not upon what is the right thing to do but upon what is personally best for them.

Decisions around resources typically involve a certain amount of risk. These leaders perceive risk as anything that threatens their position. Their fear results in either indecision or choosing against the difficult, but correct, decision. The impact cascades down throughout the company. Fear by one individual then creates friction which slows the progress of the company and hinders its movement towards excellence.

The second source of fear leading to friction comes from those that lead through intimidation. And again, while I wish this were an uncommon occurrence, reality indicates otherwise. Those who attempt to lead through intimidation maintain a fundamental absence of leadership. They may get things done and often have a reputation for doing so, but they do so at a cost. A cost that impacts morale, creativity, innovation, physiological security, and the well-being of employees. People that lead through intimidation will always preclude their company from achieving excellence.

While fear isn't an uncommon source of friction, a more common one comes from excesses. If something is a good thing, more of it isn't always better. Examples include excessive emails, meetings, and reviewers for internal approvals. If we assess these individually, each will have a different cause, but the impact would be the same—unnecessary inefficiencies that drive hidden costs into the business.

I've always believed emails to be a data repository vice a primary means of communication. Far too often an office conversation tied to miscommunication includes the phrase "I sent you an email on that."

The email serves as an artifact. It shouldn't be a replacement for actual communication. The reality of this became apparent during the 2016 Presidential campaign and the mysterious classified email server.

I once held a management position where I dealt with up to 400 emails a day. We supported operations around the clock, so this occurred over more than just an eight-hour day. But still, this was crazy. We also spent much of our day in meetings, causing a tremendous amount to catch up on each evening.

And speaking of meetings, I was an executive at a large company where top leadership viewed the time spent in meetings as some perverted badge of honor. I did the math once, just to confirm the lunacy. On average, my typical 40-hour work week included more than 50 hours of meetings. Double and triple bookings for the same time slot weren't the exception. They were the rule.

Friction induced from this situation continued for years. I attempted many fixes, to include a simple battle rhythm that pre-allocated times by meeting types with scheduled block-out time. We needed time to think— time to lead the company. Nothing I did resolved the friction. The boss liked it that way and wasn't about to change. The price paid was an impact to morale and efficiency. But more importantly, the behavior crushed creativity, time to think, and our time to strategize.

Senior leadership's love of meetings is nothing new. Taiichi Ohno, founder of the Toyota Production System, identified years ago that executives maintain different perspectives of waste relative to labor and management. Ohno explains senior executives emphasize elimination of waste from the labor process while viewing their own non-productive time, such as time spent in meetings, as sacred.

There's a growing belief among some Lean thinkers that top management is intentionally inefficient. Non-productive consumption of time can unfortunately be perceived as something earned within the executive ranks. Meetings, business travel, delayed action, and indecisiveness often have the highest importance, even if they serve the purpose of the executive over the organization.

Steve Jobs famously limited meetings to essential personnel, required that someone owned each agenda item, and refused to allow PowerPoint to drive meetings. Elon Musk insists that meetings be limited to only a few people. Richard Branson conducts most meetings standing up to limit their length. There are other positive examples. But for many of us, continuing to do what we've been doing isn't effective and only serves to hold us back from getting closer to excellence.

An overwhelming amount of data is available on the impact of poor meeting management. Yet it continues to plague our productivity. It will continue to do so until leadership at the top decides to change "the way things get done around here." Going forward, with our increased prevalence of remote work, it will be interesting to observe changes to our overall management of meetings.

My last friction example is the practice of requiring excessive approvers for internal documents. I've seen simple approvals require up to 20 signatures. It's even worse if the system is limited to serial approvals. The problem usually traces to a lack of defined roles and responsibilities. No one would intentionally require that much oversight. But as companies grow, each individual business system continues to grow organically and, over time, produces multiple complex and inefficient systems. I'll address the fix for this in Chapter 12.

Friction is best dealt with through confrontation—and lubrication.

Lubricant reduces the impact of friction between surfaces. Within our companies, these surfaces are the people that interface to complete their work. Examples of lubricant to reduce friction include:

- Managers and leaders having the moral courage to conduct difficult conversations
- Challenging the way things get done around here with calm directness
- Valuing empathy, listening, and understanding for what employees tell us
- Being intentional with how time is spent and refusing to accept mediocrity
- Identifying and removing issues at their root through effective problem-solving

I encourage people to call out friction anytime it surfaces. The worst thing we can do is accept it. Much of this friction can be corrected at the root and removed from the flow. Except of course the case of leaders not qualified to be in their positions. But like I said, that's a different conversation.

VICTIMHOOD

Our American culture is said to be saturated with victimhood, entitlement, and codependence. Of these conditions, victimhood delivers the most harm to our businesses.

Coping with constant change in today's workplace tends to increase stress. If change isn't effectively managed, frustration ensues. This frustration leads to despondency. Productivity then decreases. The final state is reached as pessimism and despair become commonplace. Such a state is full of victims. It can break a culture. And what gets broken doesn't always go back together again.

A victim culture exists when "the way things get done around here" aligns with a resounding belief of being a victim. Twenty-five years ago, a national best-seller claimed the problem to be rampant, even an epidemic, within American business. Things haven't improved.

As we move our organizations towards excellence, we must remain vigilant against victimhood. And management has no immunity. Research indicates a growing lack of enthusiasm in the management ranks, partly due to change and the demands it requires, both physiologically and psychologically. This environment becomes a petri dish for a victim culture. It exists far too often for us to be comfortable.

But we don't have to accept this as our fate. The first step to getting better is often just recognizing the problem. The following elements, when present within a culture, are indicators of victimhood:

Tendency to refuse to accept accountability	Feelings of despair, helplessness, or guilt
Absence of independent thought	Perceived traumatic setback caused by change
Constantly seeking someone else to blame	Underlying lack of self-respect
Prevalence of passive attitudes	Over-riding fear of failure

I've worked at several places mired in victimhood. For effective leaders wanting to achieve a better state for things, it's not difficult to recognize. But these aren't the people we must convince. We must show the people affected by this state the truth of the situation.

Several years ago, I was tasked to turnaround an engineering department struggling on several fronts. Executive leadership believed the unit to be dysfunctional. They charged me to change things. After assessing the situation, I sensed the presence of many victims. I worked with Human Resources to develop a leadership seminar for the department. Within the curriculum, we created a role-playing exercise intended to expose this victimhood.

During a group session with department leaders, we paired them to tell one another a work story where the result produced something other than a desired outcome. We encouraged them to relate stories with emotional connections. The narratives were lively. And often sad. And in every case related in a way that the tellers perceived themselves to be a victim.

I'll never forget the sense of helplessness in that room. After each pair told their respective stories, we had them repeat the exercise. We instructed them to retell the same stories, but for this second telling, we changed the rules.

We instructed them to assume responsibility and accountability for what they could have affected to enable a different outcome. We tasked them to retell the same story but identify what they personally could have done differently to ensure a successful result.

Fault and blame were more difficult to find. Results, ownership, and task accomplishment dominated the discussions. The mood in the room changed. The same stories were quite different this time. There were quite a few "ah hah" moments that afternoon. It was a simple exercise but produced a powerful lesson.

The most important tool for a *recovering* victim, someone that becomes aware of the truth of the situation, is a mirror. When used properly, the reflection that stares back at them is often the person most able to influence the change they desperately seek. Like the psychiatrist and philosopher Carl Jung informed us, we are not what happened to us—we are what we choose to become.

DEVIANCE

At 48,000 ft above the Florida coast, the Space Shuttle *Challenger* began to break up in flight. The nation bowed in sorrow as we watched in disbelief.

The Rogers Commission published their findings several months later, blaming the infamous O-ring. The O-ring was the *direct cause* of the incident. But it wasn't the *root cause*. Scientists knew about the faulty O-ring design for years, yet a series of management decisions resulted in NASA granting six different waivers related to O-ring launch constraints.

Ten years after the incident, sociologist Diane Vaughan published *The Challenger Launch Decision*. Vaughan coined a term tied to organizational life that more accurately identified the actual root cause. She described the "normalization of deviance" present in NASA culture where deviant behavior had become more accepted as normal with each occurrence. Over time, this deviance affected management decisions and ultimately led to the *Challenger* incident.

Normalizing deviance occurs quite often and with seemingly inconsequential actions. But the truth is, these actions cost companies untold fortunes in lost revenue.

Across many industries, creativity, ingenuity, and freedom of action are understandably more valued than conformity and compliance. But in more structured industries, such as healthcare, manufacturing, and transportation, standardized rules carry significant importance.

Our companies establish rules—policies, procedures, and standard practices—for how things get done. These rules, and our response to them, make up a big part of the culture, of "the way things get done around here." Behavior outside of these rules typically results in corrective action. Sometimes though, behavior continues to operate outside the rules without correction. Over time, this deviant behavior becomes normalized as acceptable and a one-time shortcut eventually becomes the new norm.

Deviant behavior creates latent errors that entrench within the system's architecture. These flaws remain unseen until an active error or other catalyst triggers an unplanned sequence of events.

Deviance was normalized leading up to the *Costa Concordia* capsizing. It was present at Chernobyl, Bhopal, and the BP Texas City refinery explosion. And it was present in Kentucky at the Upper Big Branch Mine. Here, officials cited the mine owner for 62,923 safety violations over ten years. The catalyst eventually revealed itself and 29 miners lost their lives.

There are many other examples. I've seen cultures overwhelmed to the point that managers develop metrics to track efficiency of behavior that is itself deviant.

In more structured industries, it's critically important to know, understand, and follow written procedures. If the procedures aren't good, change them. But we should never tolerate people just ignoring them. This is where leadership comes into play.

Three primary factors, each tied to our humanity, can lead to deviance becoming normalized as acceptable behavior:

- **Institutionalization**—leaders work around the rules or willingly tolerate others who do so
- **Socialization**—social conformity results in people adopting observed behavior or not voicing concerns about known violations
- **Rationalization**—people justify their actions for not following a rule

It's said an organization's culture is shaped by the worst behavior the leader is willing to tolerate. Leaders need to set the example, to include an unwillingness to accept the failure to follow process. Below are additional countermeasures leaders can take to keep deviance from becoming normalized:

- Instill accountability as a core value
- Require familiarity with written procedures
- Periodically revise processes to reflect current business needs
- Reward steady compliance with the same vigor as "heroism"
- Teach managers how to conduct uncomfortable conversations
- Establish a suggestion program with anonymous reporting
- Encourage speaking up and reward moral courage for doing so

When deviance becomes normalized, such as witnessed at NASA, the cost impact is often the lesser concern. The last thing we want to imagine as we board our next flight is that a work-around has replaced a formal aircraft inspection procedure.

TOXICITY

Earlier I stated people are often not aware of the culture until it's challenged, and that pursuing excellence requires we continuously challenge the culture. The change associated with these acts is a blade with two edges. On one edge, it establishes a tighter and more focused business that aligns operations to strategy. But on the other edge, it can create a backlash of distrust, unrest, and victimhood.

We've discussed how friction, victimhood, and deviance can each affect the way things get done around here. Other factors sometimes combine with these to multiply their impact. An example would be the lack of accountability becoming normalized as the accepted way things get done. The combinations can be devastating. And they often lead to what we call a toxic culture.

Internal fighting, drama, and unhappiness in our work life can degrade to the point that it affects our health. While many assume leadership is to blame, I have a different take. I believe we all play a part. Leadership sets the overall tone for what gets done, but collectively we all contribute to the culture.

Recall Schein's definition for culture as "the accumulated shared learning" that is "taught to new members as the correct way to perceive, think, feel, and behave." We each have a hand in forming the culture. And when that formation becomes toxic, we need to be accountable to ourselves and to others. This can be hard to admit, but it doesn't change its truth. Our failure to accept this truth could be because the toxicity has become so strong that it fogs our mirror and prevents us from seeing our true self.

When we problem-solve to address the cause for failures and undesired conditions, every cause can eventually be traced back to a common point. We can always blame management. That's one approach. Or instead, we can choose to be accountable for those things that we control.

Identified below are common signs that a culture has become toxic and is not effectively serving the needs of the employees, the company, or the customer. Any one probably doesn't create a toxic culture. But the combination of several very well could indicate its presence.

Potential Indicators of a Toxic Culture	
Management rewards bad behavior	Competition rises to become dysfunctional
Focus remains on short-term results	Leadership by intimidation creates fear
Lack of transparency from leadership	Undue concern for titles or positional authority
High employee turnover	Strong presence of victimhood
Excessive sick days	Open disrespect towards others
Lack of trust, up and down	Constant office gossip
Political alliances are coveted over teaming	Managers are overly ambitious to a fault
Obvious presence of normalized deviance	Lack of empathy exists across all levels
Absence of accountability	Constant presence of excessive stress
Excessive friction	Obvious jockeying for power and position

This isn't meant to be a complete list. And one of these, trust, needs to be discussed in further detail. But before that, it's interesting to note how many of these signs are errors of *commission* vice errors of *omission*. They are things people *intentionally* do. That's worth thinking about.

But now let's discuss trust and its importance to the culture. Without trust, we'll never achieve excellence. In fact, its absence results in a struggle to maintain even average performance. While trust is often perceived only as a leadership issue, this isn't the truth. Let's examine the definition to better understand.

The dictionary defines trust as having faith or confidence in something. That explanation is fine, but it fails to provide deeper understanding within our context.

Dr. Roger Mayer provides a more relevant definition as "the willingness of a party to be vulnerable to the actions of another party based on the expectation that the other will perform a particular action important to the trustor, irrespective of the ability to monitor or control that other party." Mayer's definition helps clarify that trust is a two-way street. We can blame leadership for inculcating an absence of trust, but when we do so, we may be falling into the victimhood trap. Trust goes both ways.

At the end of this book, I'll introduce stewardship as one of the fundamental leadership characteristics necessary for our companies to realize excellence, to lead with a values-based approach to leadership. Peter Block defines stewardship as "holding something in trust for another." Leaders help achieve this trust through their transformational behaviors, to include articulating a shared vision, setting the personal example, and appealing to commonly shared values.

Leaders embodying these principles are the best solution for the toxicity problem.

Companies may bring in consultants or hire externally when top leadership becomes aware of toxicity and wants change. These outsiders often don't last long. Change here is an inherently political event. The agents brought in to stimulate change can become frustrated by the system. Or they're invited to leave when the very thing they were asked to do threatens the wrong power player. A failure to make needed change here often holds lesser companies back from moving closer to excellence.

Earlier I mentioned how several of these factors can combine and truly devastate a culture. I've witnessed situations where victimhood and the absence of accountability reigned, even at senior levels.

When senior leaders deny accountability, it's pointless to expect a different behavior from subordinates. Making changes in this environment requires moral courage. It can threaten the status quo and is often resisted with concerted effort. Support from the top is required. Top leaders incur an obligation to make the difficult decisions necessary for the company to move beyond this negative behavior.

Our culture is too important to our success and too influential on our daily work life to tolerate elements we know to be wrong. Making changes here often requires leaders to challenge the culture, to challenge "the way things get done around here." Challenging the status quo can have political ramifications, but that doesn't change the need for leaders to act. This is one of the more difficult tasks for leaders, but one they cannot ignore. It is much easier to tolerate these things than to act and ensure we perform our role as leaders.

4

Clarifying Our Leadership

A Chinese proverb relates the beginning of wisdom is to call things by their proper names. Leadership is an interesting word in that many of us have different definitions that we steadfastly hold to as "our" definition. That's okay. Passion here is a good thing.

This "thing" we call leadership is all about people. The output of this idea called leadership is *influence*. Complicated definitions are sometimes fine, but they aren't necessary here. We're discussing the fundamentals of how people influence and get other people closer to the desired end-state in our environments of conflict, competition, and change.

LEADERSHIP versus MANAGEMENT

If we scanned our social media updates right now, I bet we would find a post with a cool graphic that compares leaders to managers. The graphic will likely portray leaders with self-actualized and desired skills while portraying managers as evil with controlling and mal-intended attributes.

Comparisons such as these reinforce the thought process that we must be either one thing or another—that one person cannot possess both characteristics. I'll provide more on that in a moment.

Gallup interviewed 80,000 managers to distinguish characteristics between managers and leaders. In *First, Break All the Rules*, Gallup's Marcus Buckingham and Curt Coffman informed us that great managers are not sitting around waiting for "leadership to be thrust upon them." Some, to include those at the highest executive levels, have a perception that managers and leaders are different entities. Those making such assumptions are holding back their business and its people from excellence.

All managers have varying degrees of leadership skills. And the people that we choose to characterize as leaders have management skills but also in varying degrees. While only the rare person excels in both leadership and management competencies, our companies need a collection of people with each skill.

A company comprised entirely of great leaders with poor management skills may be a wonderful place to work, but it won't be around for long. Such a company will soon be obviated by the competition. Likewise, an organization comprised of great managers with poor leadership skills would be a difficult place to work. Such a place would fall far short of excellence.

My beliefs here are founded in practical application. Fifteen years before I was awarded a master's in executive leadership, I earned the same degree in management. I've led hundreds of people while managing multi-million-dollar budgets to plan and control assets worth billions of dollars. While being a leader may be the perceived sexy role, I've learned being an effective manager is equally important.

We must seek to improve our leadership *and* our management skills. The previous statement may seem obvious. But if we continue to idolize leadership while denigrating management, we'll eventually stray from valuing what an effective manager has to offer. Take a moment to review these comparisons, pulled from popular perception, to view the apparent preference of leaders to managers.

- *Leaders build relationships; managers comply with procedures*
- *Leaders develop and empower talent; managers plan*
- *Leaders motivate and inspire; managers direct*
- *Leaders create; managers budget*
- *Leaders coach; managers evaluate*
- *Leaders build trust; managers facilitate*

Given these comparisons, who would want to be known as a manager instead of a leader?

Consider these manager roles. And now imagine working for a company that fails to plan, direct, budget, evaluate, or comply with procedures. But hurry, because that company won't be around for long.

Becoming effective at leadership and management, and therefore being both a leader and a manager, may require us to view the world differently. Life teaches us that we can't have our cake and eat it too. We're taught to believe that when examining attributes, we conduct a mental comparison and choose one over the other based upon preferences for what we value. We're led to believe that we must choose *either* one *or* the other. But *both* are often required.

Many times, the attributes being compared are polarities of the same system.

Imagine choosing between empowering and planning, motivating and directing, creating and budgeting, or coaching and evaluating. These choices are often presented within a system in which they are dependent upon one another. Our traditional mindset teaches us that we must choose one or the other. Achieving excellence requires that we value both. And that we likewise be able to choose both.

We need to adjust our thinking to prioritize *what* is important *when*. This process, known as *both/and thinking*, requires that we take a different approach to the constraints of time and perspective. Such thoughts form the heart of the Competing Values Framework.

Shedding the time constraint allows us to decide when to lead and when to manage. Shedding the perspective constraint allows us to open our aperture and consider that we can be both. We can be *both* a manager *and* a leader. Leadership and management are different. We all get that. And one isn't better or more important than the other. But each is more important at specific moments and places.

Leadership requires a certain reciprocal act from others. The most advanced form of leadership is that of a servant nature. Robert Greenleaf informs us the only real test of leadership is that somebody follows. I'll discuss more about this in the Epilogue.

Management doesn't typically require the same reciprocal relationship. Acts here tend to be unidirectional. But management has many tests, the results of which can be found in some particularly important places, like a company's financial statements and balance sheet.

LEADERSHIP STYLE

My undergraduate degree is in physics. Some may believe this to be a difficult subject. But with physics, a problem has a single true answer. All other solutions are false. Equations and formulas help us find the answer to the problem.

Leadership isn't so simple. There's no formula to apply and there's seldom a single answer. The preferred leadership style advocated most appropriate to realizing excellence is situational, by definition.

In 1969, Paul Hersey and Ken Blanchard put forth their "Life Cycle Theory of Leadership" in *Management of Organizational Behavior*. By the book's third edition, they renamed their ideas to situational leadership theory. As time progressed, each author developed their own model with slight variations, but the underlying ideas remain consistent.

The essence of situational leadership theory is embedded in our corporate leadership training curriculums. I was first exposed to the theory 25 years ago while pursuing my first graduate degree. Fifteen years later, I had the fortune to study under Ken Blanchard and then certify under Paul Hersey's team. I'm convinced insight from this theory has been key to any success I've achieved.

The central tenant of situational leadership theory is "It depends." The theory professes there's no single best leadership approach for all situations. The leader focuses attention on the follower to determine the most appropriate leadership style. The underlying essence is that people vary in development for explicit tasks and require different leadership behaviors dependent upon the follower's development.

Assuming the follower as the independent variable, the leader applies a style commensurate to the follower's development level in that task. A leader adopts one of four styles, based upon the individual's competency and commitment in the specific task.

We have many different approaches for leadership. Some are quite effective. Others not so much. Experience and wisdom help us differentiate. I chose to mention situational leadership due to its strong correlation to leading people through the change present when pursuing excellence.

But I'm under no illusion that there aren't other approaches and styles that can also deliver effective results.

Rather than examine other styles here, or continue exploring situational leadership in more detail, I want to pivot. Formal leadership training provides deeper insight to the various theories, such as situational leadership. Most of these serve to make us more effective. Being more effective in our leadership is surely one of the keys to achieving excellence. But the most important leadership characteristics aren't things we are taught.

Most leaders wear many hats. Let's play on that concept and discuss HAT leadership as the hidden ingredient that determines a leader's overall success. Here the acronym HAT refers to *humility, authenticity,* and *transparency.*

Just like we don't set out to *implement* Operational Excellence, but rather we *achieve* it through realizing an improved state of performance, we don't make a plan to become humble, authentic, or transparent. These aren't traits we turn on and off and sometimes decide to be, or not be. They're qualities that characterize the essence of how we see ourselves and how others see us within our human value system.

These things we're discussing are key to moving our companies from average to excellent. Most companies will be average, by definition. Similarly, the people that lead others within our companies will also trend towards average.

But most people don't believe themselves to be average. This is especially true when the measured characteristic is something personally valued, such as the planning competencies of managers or the analysis capabilities of engineers. The higher up in positional authority, the less those measured tend to envision themselves as average. Yet the principles of statistics remain valid.

Interesting studies have queried large groups of CEOs to get their perceived ranking against other CEOs. Not surprisingly, the overwhelming *majority* believe themselves to be *above average*. Do we just chalk this up to confidence or is it indicative of some other self-awareness issue? To explore this further, we need to return to the concept of humility.

Confidence is an important characteristic for those who lead others, especially through change. To lack confidence is to be timid and full of doubt, not something we seek in our leaders. There's a fine line between confidence and arrogance. We don't seek arrogance in our leaders, although it remains present far too often. The opposite of arrogance is humility, something we do seek in our leaders, but something which is too frequently absent.

Humility is an attribute recognized in our most successful leaders. Trends in the data inform us that leaders who under-rate themselves on leadership effectiveness are rated highest by direct reports. And leaders who overrate themselves are often perceived by direct reports to be low in both self-awareness and effectiveness. These trends are telling us something—and that something is about humility.

Here's the unique thing about humility. Those lacking in this area, that have essentially no humility and couldn't care less about being humble, possess a fundamental absence of leadership. They may even brag about their humility. This simply underscores they don't get it. For these people, we can coach them, provide them mentors, and give them leadership books to read. Most of them won't change. And actions to try and do so are far beyond the scope of this book.

Near equal to the importance of humility is the need for leaders to be authentic. Authenticity is presenting our self as we are—coming from a real place within. We are authentic when our actions and our words are congruent with our values and our beliefs. It means being who we are, not falsely portraying to be something we think we should be or what others tell us we should be. A leader who is authentic approaches their work in a truthful and transparent manner through humility and accountable behavior. It sounds simple enough, but it's another trait absent far too often in our leaders.

And transparency, like authenticity and humility, is another characteristic that forms the essence of who a leader is, and how they view the world. A leader who approaches their work with transparency quickly gains the trust of subordinates and seniors alike. A transparent leader emphasizes openness and persuasion over control. For our senior leaders, running the company with transparent behavior does more to build trust than any other action.

Our test for this transparency is when employees no longer feel the need to hide information. When we arrive at this point, they will share both good news and bad with the same velocity.

As I stated earlier, these important leadership characteristics aren't things that we're taught. But they can be honed by the right environment.

Marine Corps Officer Candidate School (OCS) provides such a crucible to help identify those possessing these characteristics and those who do not. The program doesn't train young men and women to be Marine officers. Instead, the mission of Marine OCS is to "evaluate and screen individuals for the leadership, moral, mental and physical qualities required for commissioning as a Marine Corps officer."

The selection process just to attend OCS is quite restrictive. Once a class convenes, the historical attrition rate exceeds 35 percent. The result is a "controlled and challenging environment" that effectively removes those without the mettle to lead.

The recent challenges we've all worked through with the coronavirus highlight the real value of leadership. The situation presented anything but a "controlled" environment.

We all saw people respond by stepping up and leading others through the challenge. We also saw some leaders go absent for days or weeks.

I've completed training designed to challenge your physical and psychological limits while observing your ability to lead. The training broke some people. Some failed to rise above the challenge and perform the duties of a leader. We referred to this as cocooning up—inverting all thoughts, energy, and emotions inward. Such action may be acceptable for an individual not responsible for others. But it is never acceptable for a leader, whether in a uniform or a business suit.

Most every decent book on leadership recognizes the importance of these characteristics. There's enough already written on the subject that I won't further delay our discussion here. But I do want to underscore their importance with this: a company will never achieve excellence if those at the top do not lead with these values-based characteristics.

MANAGEMENT SKILLS

For a long time, we've believed to know the skills needed to manage our companies. The way we used to do this may no longer apply going forward. Managing for success in our new world will require new ideas and approaches to our fundamental business constructs.

The predominant approach to managing business, according to classical management based upon social, moral, and economic philosophies, has remained mostly unchanged since the 18th century. Since then, different philosophies have come and gone, but the ideas for what it takes to manage a company towards success have remained fairly constant, although often given different names.

The Scientific Management approach was the new thing from 1890 through about 1940. Following this movement, the world engaged in a terrible war that would dominate thoughts and innovation over the next decade. Then a series of events happened that would change how many of us perceive our roles.

In 1950, while helping rebuild the Japanese economy, General McArthur invited Dr. Edward Deming to Japan to speak to their leading industrialists. Japanese industry would soon transform.

And in 1955, social psychologist Robert L. Katz published an article identifying the emphasis of skills across different management levels. Katz's work is generally recognized as insightful, but I believe it's underappreciated for what it helps us understand.

Since then, we've experienced different initiatives targeting improvement, to include Total Quality Management (TQM), Toyota Production System (TPS), Lean, Six Sigma, and Lean Six Sigma. And as discussed earlier, each returned moderate success, at best. But within the United States, they haven't delivered successful transformation to mid-size and larger companies. And there's a reason. A reason that traces back to the insight provided by Katz.

Katz's theory helps us understand our focus as we progress from managing our team to our function to our business. The model shows us the different emphasis on technical, human, and conceptual skills needed at each level.

Back in Chapter 1, I introduced two reasons why Lean and Six Sigma haven't been successful leading transformational change needed to achieve excellence. We touched on the first reason, not gaining buy-in from senior leaders, before examining the second reason, not gaining buy-in from those affected by the change.

Now I want to return to that first reason these methodologies have struggled. Simply put, most senior leaders remain inclined *not* to embrace these modern continuous improvement efforts.

When McArthur brought Deming to Japan, companies didn't delegate attendance to engineers or operational managers. The company leaders attended. And in doing so, which is central to their culture, they set the precedence for how Deming's principles would be embraced in Japan. The same behavior isn't paralleled in American business. And Katz's model helps us understand why.

Using the Katz model as a base, we can expand these ideas to see our approach to management, problem-solving, and improvement as indicated in Figure 4.1.

Expanding on Katz's theory, we see top management focuses on managing the business while leaving management of process to middle and front-line managers. Similarly, top management isn't concerned with solving technical problems. They focus on problems thought to be impeding the business.

We shouldn't be surprised by top management's lack of buy-in to the technical aspect of managing process through the tools offered by Lean and Six Sigma. But we also see how Operational Excellence *can be* in the

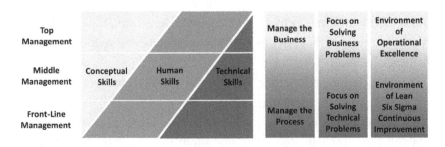

FIGURE 4.1

Management skills by level. (Adapted from Katz's *Skills of an Effective Administrator*.)

realm of top management through adjusting our lens and how we frame the problem.

Study Figure 4.1 for a moment. There's a lot of information here, and most of it is common sense. But until we view these things through such an image, the whole picture may not be apparent.

Conceptualization is a role largely limited to top leaders. Focus shifts to human and technical skills as we move down the chain. The most effective executive leaders appreciate these different perspectives for how we approach work. Those leading from a values-based approach understand they must seek a delicate balance between conceptual thinking and a day-to-day operational approach.

Recall our earlier discussion on flow kaizen and its emphasis on enterprise-level value stream improvements. American companies haven't embraced this idea. And again, there's a reason.

Senior leaders prefer the familiar. They prefer those things which they already have expertise and therefore don't have to expose ignorance or give up any perceived referent power. They maintain a certain level of discomfort with these foreign ideas of kaizen, kanban, and gemba. This introduces a hidden problem. It's a problem that has kept most mid-size and larger companies from fully deploying Lean or Lean Six Sigma to help facilitate transformation. But framing the problem within an Operational Excellence context can provide us the needed solution.

Managers and directors operate in a world of concrete reality, of facts and data that are based on cause-and-effect relationships. The skills needed to thrive in this environment focus on human and technical skills, with little emphasis on conceptual skills. As middle managers, they're responsible for executing the strategy of senior leadership. Returning to senior leadership isn't uncommon, either to brief them on status or seek direction on strategy execution.

These briefs between senior leaders and middle managers can often become frustrating experiences.

Senior leaders prefer to hear conclusions that play to their confirmation bias and support their preconceptions about the genius of their strategy. They're far less concerned about data and facts than they are about higher order business concepts that support their vision. The disconnect between briefer and receiver can often be a chasm. Each has beliefs about what is important that prevent one from fully understanding the other. Eventually frustration sets in, and nothing is achieved.

Nothing is achieved until both sides change their mindset. Middle managers need to learn to appreciate the top management's conceptual world and change how they frame their message. And top management need to remember where they came from and appreciate the fact-based cause-and-effect work of middle management. This type of compromise is a continual and mandatory path on the journey to excellence.

Advanced application of situational leadership helps uncover the root cause why senior leaders push back against adopting new principles, such as Lean Six Sigma. The basis of situational leadership is that people have varying degrees of competence and commitment for all skills. When senior leaders openly demonstrate resistance to these new ideas, there's a good chance they're masking their lack of competence with an aggressive posture that appears as a lack of commitment. They argue against the ideas because they fear their lack of competence in something new.

Marshall Goldsmith's brilliant book *What Got You Here Won't Get You There* provides even more insight. This book helped us understand the skills that brought us success at our current level aren't the same skills needed at the next level. This applies to individuals and to companies. The practices, behaviors, and thought processes that got the company to average performance are not the same practices, behaviors, and thought processes that will get it to excellent performance.

DECISION-MAKING

Most companies understand the importance of executive decision quality. But the same logic doesn't hold for middle and front-line management decisions. Middle managers and front-line managers don't make strategic decisions that establish direction for the company. I understand that. Yet they make everyday decisions to execute and implement strategic direction. Poor tactical decisions during execution can have equally devastating impact as any bad strategic decision.

Most business schools include at least one course in decision-making. These don't fully meet our needs. The courses tend to focus on improving skills for data-driven decisions. While skills in analysis are important, many of the decisions facing leaders are often more dependent upon their judgment and interpretation of emotions than the ability to interpret statistical data. Still other decisions only present themselves through synthesis of data—something we'll discuss in Chapter 6.

We have discussed the importance of beliefs and how these beliefs are based on our underlying assumptions. Our assumptions directly impact our decision-making. We often must make decisions in the absence of complete information. Sometimes, the assumptions we make are wrong. That's unavoidable. But our approach must include the appropriate rigor to frequently revisit and validate our assumptions. We'll discuss more on this in the problem-solving discussion later in the book.

Ultimately, we're looking to improve our ability to make accurate and timely decisions. Many factors influence and affect this ability.

There's a thought process that our intuition and judgment are based on our emotion-laden moral beliefs. Specifically, our intuition provides an immediate emotional response that helps us understand what we should do, then our moral judgment attempts to analyze, understand, and rationalize a course of action. We *can* improve our judgment and intuition. We do so through experience and insight drawn from our values, beliefs, emotions, and awareness of the variables in play.

Learning through experience often means getting some things wrong before getting them right. To counter this, several sense-making applications are available to help us make better decisions faster.

A theory associated with learning, introduced in Chapter 3, describes the four stages of competence. A shortcut to arrive at the highest form of competence, *unconscious competence*, is to apply a memory mnemonic so our thought process is memorized and applied automatically.

We face an incredible number of decisions each day—some more important than others. Our brains develop shortcuts that recognize patterns and help simplify the analytical thought required to make these decisions. If we didn't have these mental shortcuts, we would regularly be frozen by indecision.

We can intentionally design these shortcuts using heuristics to help our brain process information needed to make routine decisions. Taken from the Greek language "to discover," heuristics provide shortcuts that reduce the signals sent to the brain to analyze alternatives and arrive at a decision.

One of my favorite heuristics is the OODA loop. Developed by Colonel John Boyd to help fighter pilots make quicker decisions, the OODA loop, shown in Figure 4.2, helps us complete rapid mental steps to arrive at a decision.

The first step of OODA is to **O**bserve what's going on through every means available to the senses. The next step is to **O**rient our self to *synthesize* the data and develop a mental perspective. Next, **D**ecide on the course of action to pursue. The final step is to **A**ct on the decision. The process is continuous, so as soon as we **A**ct, the situation changes, and we return to **O**bserve to repeat the process.

The power of the OODA loop and its non-linear learning is that as we begin to use it, our brain becomes conditioned to subconsciously apply the process. We're continuously observing the environment, orienting our self, making decisions, acting, and then re-assessing the acted-upon environment. The process becomes a powerful but unconscious mental heuristic. In other words, it becomes a habit.

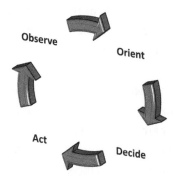

FIGURE 4.2
OODA loop.

The OODA loop works independent of the decision timeframe. Boyd designed the model for fighter pilots making decisions measured in seconds. But the model works where decisions vary from days to weeks and even months.

While Boyd is best known for the OODA loop that helped improve pilot performance in the Korean War, he was a thought leader and accomplished innovator. He studied many other thought leaders, to include the founders of the Toyota Production System, Shigeo Shingo and Taiichi Ohno. The Marine Corps University Archives in Quantico, VA, house many of Boyd's personal books. Boyd's frequent writings in the book margins provide insight to his thoughts. These personal notes reveal Boyd's fundamental belief in the importance of people and ideas over tools, systems, and hardware.

Tools to improve our decision-making vary from simple models such as the OODA loop to detailed statistical decision trees assigning weighted values to probability-driven events. More important than any model or heuristic is the need to invest intentional thought into making our decisions. When doing so, we must acknowledge that we spend significantly more time dealing with the consequences of our decisions than we invested into making them in the first place.

OODA and other similar heuristics can help us make faster and better decisions. But in our work life as it has become, we're often overwhelmed with information and the apparent need to make an ever-increasing number of decisions.

A lot of this is noise and distracts us from what's important. Two proven tools can help us cut through this noise. And we need to do so. We need to focus our energy on the things that if we fix, can help move our companies towards excellence.

Steven Covey re-introduced the business world to the Eisenhower decision matrix. The matrix is simple, but powerful. It helps us prioritize tasks between those that are important and those that are not. And it helps us identify false priorities. While most of us are familiar with the matrix as shown in Figure 4.3, I'm not convinced we apply it, or another methodology, to help ensure we focus on the correct priorities.

FIGURE 4.3

Eisenhower decision matrix.

When used as part of our normal routine, we often find that we're pulled to spend more time on urgent tasks than we spend on important tasks. That should cause us concern.

In the early stages of the coronavirus pandemic, companies faced decisions whether to continue with the status quo or suspend operations. Leaders assessed each decision for the risk and reward, which in many cases often meant deciding whether to just continue normal operations.

I applied the decision matrix to help guide my decisions and those of my team. The simple tool provided valuable insight to discriminate between those tasks we had to do immediately and those that could wait. It's an interesting irony that the crisis helped clarify false priorities while providing time to plan and decide for those tasks determined to be important but not urgent.

Another powerful and well-documented tool to help us make better and faster decisions is the Pareto Principle, or 80/20 rule. Entire books have been written on this subject, and some of them are quite good. The essence of the principle is that 80 percent of what we should care about is driven from only 20 percent of the causes. The 80/20 rule helps us focus our energy on the things that matter most.

A cautionary note may be prudent. Some people mis-apply the Pareto Principle and believe that it drives us to an 80 percent solution. The principle advocates no such thing. What it does advocate is providing our full energy to developing a complete solution for those few causes that generate most of our problems. This allows us to optimize resources so we can continue to move towards excellence.

We optimize our effectiveness by ignoring 80 percent of the causes to focus on the few that matter most. We have finite time to deal with the issues we face in our daily work life. We could even say that we face an issue of time bankruptcy.

Someone I'm quite fond of likes to use time as an excuse for not accomplishing given tasks. Truth be told, I also find myself wanting more time as the pace of life continuously increases. But this excuse has no validity.

The time it takes the Earth to make one revolution has been constant for quite a few years. We all have the same amount of time in each day as Leonardo De Vinci, Mother Teresa, and Mahatma Gandhi were each provided. The allocation of time is clearly not in our control. What is in our control is how we choose to spend that time.

Time is constant and is constantly moving forward. Some even say it flies. Michael Altshuler reminds us of the good news in that we are the pilot. Applying the Pareto Principle and Eisenhower decision matrix can help us become more effective pilots and make better decisions for how we allocate our time.

These simple tools identify tasks and causes that I've declared we should ignore. Ignoring those tasks and causes will present some risk. We need to be okay with that.

And the reason we can be okay with that is because pursuing excellence requires that we continually apply risk-based thinking within our strategy and our daily routine. This will be discussed more in Chapter 6 when we explore the systems and structures that make up our companies.

5

Aligning Our Strategy

Luck has been described as the product of preparation and opportunity. A company's strategy shouldn't come about through luck—it should come about through planning and intentional actions. This one's important, so I'll repeat it. A strategy comes from planning and intentional actions.

The need to define strategy has always been important. But in our new world, the effectiveness that we translate strategy into action will separate the companies that survive from those that don't.

A company's strategic plan is the product of the strategic planning process. As a process and not an event, this isn't a once and done thing. The most important part of planning isn't the product of the effort—it's the intentional process of getting there.

Intentional actions come from being intentional, through intentionality. But we don't use the word intentionality enough. Some even believe it to be a philosopher's word. We need to expand its use beyond those who ponder the nature of existence. Buddhists believe intentionality creates karma. At its root, karma means "intentional action." When we are intentional, clarity of purpose becomes apparent. For a company, being intentional leads to the vision and what the company seeks to become.

ALIGNMENT

Alignment is the resulting product realized from the vision, mission, values, and beliefs statements. It reflects everybody rowing in the same direction. An organization in near-perfect alignment can leverage this strength to make up for other system weaknesses. And conversely, gaps in alignment can signal problems in either the vision, mission, or beliefs statement that form the essence of the company.

Alignment is critical *within* the executive team, *between* the executive team and middle management, and then *down* through the supervisory ranks and front-line workers. A lack of alignment in any of these areas *will* work against the fiber of the organization.

Alignment towards a unified direction in strategy, goals, and objectives can be especially challenging in the presence of strong subcultures.

I once served in a company that lacked any semblance of executive team alignment. Strong subcultures were firmly in place. The alignment problem carried downstream and created similar issues throughout the company. Everyone was aware of the problem, yet it continued for years before leadership finally took decisive action. Instead of attacking the root of the issue, senior leaders continually chose to attack symptom after symptom.

They spent millions of dollars on surveys, consultants, and process improvement initiatives. These struggled to return fractional improvements. And they were always fleeting. The problem wasn't corrected until the senior team looked themself in the mirror and admitted they were the problem.

A lack of alignment tends to be poorly camouflaged. People sense its presence from the increased friction. There are some obvious indicators that people aren't rowing in the same direction. Examples include the following signals: people fail to voice their opinion when asked; issues previously believed to be resolved continually resurface; absence of accountability and ownership; and small issues often digress into larger unsolvable issues.

Like planning, maintaining alignment isn't a singular event. It's a continual process. Changes to the culture, organizational construct, vision, mission, values, and beliefs all can, and do, affect our common orientation. And most important to our discussion is this truth: a company won't achieve excellence until the different leadership layers are aligned in their mission and purpose.

Many know the story. In 1962, a year after challenging the nation to put a man on the moon, President Kennedy was touring the NASA Space Center. He allegedly took a wrong turn and came upon a janitor cleaning a hallway. The President introduced himself and asked the man what he did at NASA. The man famously told Kennedy that he was helping put a man on the moon. Such beliefs are the embodiment of organizational alignment.

Some deny the truth of this story, discounting it as folklore. I choose to believe it's true. But no one can deny the alignment within NASA and the results that culminated in the events of July 16, 1969.

GOALS AND OBJECTIVES

We can classify goals and objectives into two broad categories—activity-based and outcome-based. Our American business culture is very results oriented, so we should expect our goals and objectives to be based on outcomes. Reality indicates otherwise.

Instead, our goals and objectives tend to be based on activity. This is common for Japanese culture, but Western culture doesn't value process with the same regard, resulting in a disconnect between our goals and what is truly valued within the organization.

Within our American culture, results are what matter. We emphasize the ends while acknowledging the means. Under Japanese management, the means are emphasized while the ends are acknowledged. Activity-based goals deliver desired results in Japan. They do not in the United States.

In our Western business culture, activity-based goals result in a workforce unclear of how their work connects to others and impacts the enterprise level.

People need to understand how their work ties to larger goals. The activity-based goal to "develop a plan to improve customer satisfaction" lacks a tangible result. Changing this to the outcome-based version of "eliminate late customer deliveries within ninety days" establishes the necessary linkage.

When President Kennedy challenged America, he didn't ask us to work harder to win the space race against the Soviet Union. If he had, that would have been an activity-based goal. Instead, Kennedy established the outcome-based goal that "this nation should commit itself to achieving the goal, before the decade is out, of landing a man on the moon and returning him safely to the earth."

The linkage between experiences, beliefs, actions, and goals is much clearer through outcome-based goals. Understanding how the culture moves from the current to the desired state towards excellence requires that we understand how the company learns. This takes us back to understanding how experiences and underlying assumptions evolve into new beliefs.

Our earlier discussion stressed the importance of creating a beliefs statement. We're seeking to define a *new* way that things get done around here. This beliefs statement becomes critical when anticipating the desired culture and how we want things to get done.

To influence the culture towards excellence, we move beyond the results, actions, and espoused beliefs to impact these underlying assumptions and experiences. Through this approach, and changing the way people think, we can achieve breakthrough performance to "the way things get done around here."

Later in the book, we'll discuss how we measure that performance and monitor it through Key Performance Indicators (KPIs). But for now, I want to keep us singularly focused on establishing these breakthrough goals and objectives.

Clarification may be necessary on the nuances between goals and objectives. While many of us use them interchangeably, an academician would typically argue a goal is an end-state we're trying to reach, and an objective is the measure of progress along the way. We can think of goals as the *end* and objectives as the *means* to get there.

President Kennedy understood the importance of breakthrough goals and the destination he was challenging us to reach. Kennedy's same speech to Congress recognized the need to do things differently when he admitted, "We have never specified long-range goals on an urgent time schedule, or managed our resources and our time so as to insure their fulfillment."

Kennedy challenged us to move out of our comfort zone. He was challenging us for breakthrough performance. This same type of energy is required to move our companies towards excellence. We do this by establishing breakthrough goals that cascade down from the company's strategic plan.

Establishing breakthrough goals to achieve higher performance is foundational to becoming operationally excellent. Remember, average is a learned behavior—we're looking to move far beyond average. And just like Operational Excellence must be championed from the top, establishing breakthrough goals also starts at the very top of the company.

Breakthrough goals typically target objectives that measure three to five years of improvement. They should instill a certain level of discomfort, and excitement, for those responsible for their pursuit. And they require different thought processes to achieve.

We're not looking to transition what we currently do. We're looking to transform what we do. We're not looking to make minor adjustments to what is; we're looking to create what isn't. Achieving breakthrough goals requires changes to the way the company operates.

Remember the truism that what we measure, improves. When we measure the efforts of breakthrough performance achieved through new ways of thinking, things significantly improve.

Let's examine Steve's business, a mid-size muffler bearing company. Last year, Steve had decent earnings and generated $100 M in revenue. He's trying to grow, so he sets a goal to increase revenue by ten percent this year. As the year progresses, he realizes some wins and losses but falls short of the target, generating sales of $108 M. He repeats the process for the following year, establishing a goal of $120 M.

The automobile after-market booms in this second year and he earns revenues of $135 M. Steve repeats the process, but for the third year, he's hesitant to try and improve upon such great performance. He decides to replicate the previous year's sales and sets a goal of $135 M. But momentum is lost. The competition erodes his market and the third year produces revenue of only $125 M.

Over these three years, Steve grew sales from $100 M to $125 M or 25 percent. Statistics from the muffler bearing industry show that over the same three years, the average increase in revenue was 23–28 percent. Steve and his company succeeded in achieving average performance.

Steve had one good year out of three. Any company can have one good year. It takes an intentional plan to achieve sustainable growth year over year.

But what if Steve took a different approach? What if he challenged his company to think differently? What would happen if he established breakthrough goals to raise performance beyond that which they had grown comfortable?

Breakthrough goals, like organizational change, trace their root back to one of two paths, *needs* and *ideas*. Let's assume Steve hires a marketing guru with new ideas to transform the way they market their muffler bearings. She sells Steve on her concept, and together with his senior leadership team, they decide to move beyond average and establish breakthrough revenue goals. They develop a three-year plan to double sales, from $100 M to $200 M.

Let's revisit the same three-year period to see how things could be different.

In the first year, reaping some early benefits from new ways of thinking about marketing, Steve's company generates revenue of $120 M. For the second year, they exploit these new ideas to open new markets. Capitalizing on the booming auto after-market in that second year, they return a whopping $170 M in revenue. And with these new markets and new ideas, the company doesn't experience the same downturn in the third year and produces sales of $196 M.

Through approaching the problem differently and establishing breakthrough goals, Steve grew the business 96 percent versus the industry average of 25 percent. I'll return to this story shortly to show a representative example and plan with more detail how this growth could indeed be possible.

ORGANIZATIONAL STRATEGY

As a caveat to the importance of this ensuing discussion, we must remember the truth that culture eats strategy for breakfast. We can't ignore culture—it's in our face every day. It demands our attention. Failure to pay it the proper attention will quickly change how we manage our priorities.

Strategy though, still of significant importance, is apparently much easier to ignore.

The above is a tongue-in-cheek statement. We all recognize the importance of strategy or we wouldn't be reading this book. But taking the time to document this strategy, and share it with those responsible for executing it, is somewhat of a rare event. A documented strategy is possibly the greatest held secret within our companies.

Dave Ramsey likes to advise his listeners that we stumble into debt over years of poor decisions, but we never stumble out of debt. We only get out of debt through intentional actions.

Similarly, companies often stumble around trying to figure out what works and avoiding what does not. But they never stumble upon a strategy to focus where they're going. Strategy is something documented through planning and intentional actions. Or rather, it's something that *should be* documented through planning and intentional actions. It's also something that's hard to do. If it weren't, it wouldn't be so difficult to find documented strategies that establish the path forward for our businesses.

Most companies create mission statements that help define why they exist. Many of these companies also generate vision statements that define what they want to be. And as discussed earlier, far fewer document both their values and beliefs through a statement that describes what they value, what they believe in, and how they behave.

These three documents, the mission statement, vision statement, and the values and beliefs statement, form three of the four elements for the company's foundation. The fourth is the strategy statement—the intentional action to define the competitive game plan to achieve the vision.

I've worked for some very good companies. But I've seen few of them document a strategy statement. While these were solid companies, most were still something short of excellent. One of the more important reasons for this was their failure to document a formal strategy statement that aligned the organization to how it planned to achieve its vision.

There are three elements to a strategy statement: (1) establishing the objective; (2) clarifying the scope; and (3) defining the competitive advantage. Establishing the objective explains the end that the strategy is intended to achieve within a specified timeframe. Clarifying the scope establishes the domain of the business—the landscape in which the company operates. Defining the competitive advantage demonstrates actions that will be different from what was previously done to achieve the vision.

Many companies understand their competitive advantage. Far fewer document it. Writing it down helps define our intent. And it allows us to share the ideas with those responsible for execution. Defining the competitive advantage entails stating the value proposition and mapping how it separates us from the competition. We outline the key activities which allow us to deliver value to our customer. Then we map our high-level business model that connects these activities—from our company's inputs, through our internal processes, to the value delivered to the customer.

Documenting a strategy is important. Executing it is an entirely different thing. Companies with a formal strategy execution process outperform those without. Senior executives consistently rank *strategy execution* as one of their top priorities. While they may verbalize this as one of their top objectives, when it comes to strategy execution, we often fail to see the words followed by tangible actions.

A collective review of relevant studies reveals less than half of our companies link strategy execution to budgets. And less than a third relate strategy execution to compensation. And not surprisingly, many companies fail to explain their strategy to employees. Less than ten percent of employees admit to understanding their company's strategy. This is understandable, especially when we consider up to 90 percent of executive teams spend less than an hour each month discussing strategy.

Operational leaders are consumed by the need to achieve short-term goals. Senior leaders approach organizational problems from a conceptualizing perspective that looks beyond day-to-day realities. A values-based leader seeking to achieve excellence goes beyond conceptual thinking to also spend time developing a plan for strategy execution.

Seventy percent of companies that implement an intentional strategy execution process outperform their peers. Let's now examine how we can move from a documented strategy to tangible actions that can help us realize the strategy and, therefore, move much closer to excellence.

STRATEGIC GOAL DEPLOYMENT

Effective strategic planning moves from conceptualizing the strategy to implementation. It requires we develop solutions that coalesce operational and business processes to provide improved agility, efficiency, and responsiveness. And there's a wonderful method to help us reach this state.

One of my favorite tools associated with the Lean enterprise is the hoshin kanri planning process, often referred to as either Policy Deployment or Strategic Goal Deployment. I prefer the term Strategic Goal Deployment or SGD for short.

Unlike most Lean tools that focus on tactical improvements, SGD is a strategic tool. It guides us towards excellence by providing focus, alignment, transparency, and accountability that flows from the strategic plan down to individual employee actions. A top-down approach to drive cultural change, SGD helps ensure strategic goals align actions and improvement at every level.

Senior Managers can sometimes hold their planning role too close. SGD helps overcome this through the flow down and deployment that involves all levels as participants in the strategic planning process.

While senior management mandate the goals, the communication isn't one way. The leadership team communicate these down the chain and facilitate feedback back up the chain. This process, known as "catchball," is critical to successful execution and helps gain buy-in to the strategic plan.

Developing and then cascading goals down requires a systems approach to decision-making. In the end, we're most concerned with the net effect of how the goals work together and help us achieve the vision.

Among the various tools and methodologies discussed throughout this book, this one is possibly the most practical for helping move towards excellence. It aligns a company to a common strategy focused on breakthrough objectives and moves the corporate strategy out from the shadows of the boardroom.

The SGD process is typically ten general steps executed over the year, as indicated below:

Step 1: Establish (or reconfirm) the vision, mission, values and beliefs, and strategy statements

Step 2: Develop the three- to five-year *Breakthrough Objectives*

Step 3: Define *Annual Objectives* to accomplish this year

Step 4: Identify key processes that drive *Annual Improvement Priorities*

Step 5: Establish specific and measurable *Targets to Improve*

Step 6: Cascade objectives down through Action Plans to employees

Step 7: Execute against the *Targets to Improve* and Action Plans, affect countermeasures as needed

Step 8: Conduct monthly performance reviews

Step 9: Conduct an annual review and reflect on performance

Step 10: Revisit the strategy statement and *Breakthrough Objectives* and modify, as required

Using SGD is not complicated, but each step is essential to creating a plan that aligns the organization towards its goals. Like introduction of the Competing Values Framework earlier, the nuances of this process cannot be covered within a subchapter of any leadership book. But the ideas can be introduced to bring awareness to a powerful methodology that can help our companies on their path to excellence.

We typically document SGD in a spreadsheet referred to as the X Matrix, as shown in Figure 5.1. As its use gains popularity, vendors are developing software to assist in tracking goals and countermeasure plans. The simple spreadsheet works just as good. The tool itself won't change anything. The thought processes and actions we put into it will.

This methodology creates a data-driven structure that converts strategy into reality. It provides focus, transparency, and alignment so that everyone in the company knows the score. The objectives drive improvements to core processes, those things that must be done exceptionally well to maintain our competitive advantage.

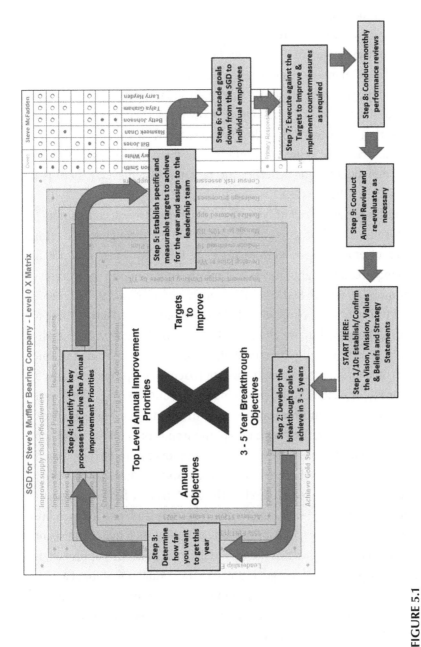

FIGURE 5.1

SGD X matrix.

As we orient to the X Matrix, clock positions are used to identify the four main elements of the matrix: *Breakthrough Objectives* are at 6 o'clock; *Annual Objectives* are at 9 o'clock; *Top Level Improvement Priorities* are at 12 o'clock; and *Targets to Improve* are at 3 o'clock.

The *Targets to Improve* are like SMART objectives and are assigned to members of the leadership team. Standard doctrine calls for using a solid dot to indicate primary responsibility for each priority. Multiple people could be supporting the objective, shown on the matrix with hollow dots.

After building the matrix, the objective owner (solid dot assignee) develops an Action Plan to track milestones and performance over the year. By SGD doctrine, we score each month's performance as either RED or GREEN, dependent upon whether the target was achieved. There is no YELLOW, only RED or GREEN. It is binary, by design.

The regular review of monthly performance helps drive accountability for that performance. The process ensures accountability through forced ratings and the requirement for countermeasure plans for all RED performance. But this also requires a thought process that may be unfamiliar to some leaders.

Accountability within SGD requires leaders not overreact to RED scores. We need to learn to be okay with RED as we remind ourselves these are challenging targets. But we *shouldn't* be okay if those things impeding progress aren't thoroughly investigated, reported, and addressed through a countermeasure plan. Through this approach, SGD provides transparency. It provides visibility into problems and resolution by driving to root cause and applying countermeasures to return to desired performance.

International corporations with tens of thousands of employees can apply SGD. Small companies with several dozen employees can also employ the tool. SGD adds value to both size companies and all those in between. A small company may have one level of the X Matrix. A larger corporation could have five or more levels; one for the corporate staff, one for each business area, and one for each major function or site. But each matrix must align back to the master X Matrix at the corporate level. With this approach, the tool aligns corporate strategic goals down to individual operational actions.

The flow down that facilitates alignment is represented in Figure 5.2. Here we see how the strategic goals cascade down to become the objectives, or means, for achieving these goals.

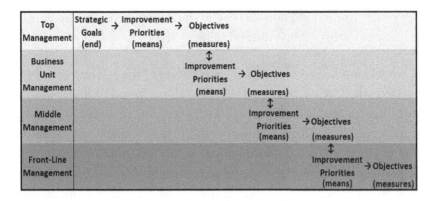

FIGURE 5.2

Alignment through SGD.

Let's return to Steve's muffler bearing company to see an example of SGD in action. Assume Steve takes the following steps to support the second scenario, where he challenges his leadership team to move beyond average:

- They establish a *Breakthrough Objective* at 6 o'clock to double sales to $200 M in three years.
- They create an *Annual Objective* at 9 o'clock to reach $120 M in sales for the first year.
- They develop an *Annual Improvement Priority* at 12 o'clock to "Incorporate new thinking in engineering to facilitate innovation."
- After catchball with the engineering team, they set a *Target to Improve* at 3 o'clock as "Implement a process for design thinking and pilot with a customer by year-end."

The VP of Engineering owns this *Target to Improve*. He cascades the goal down to his team, providing specifics for products, customers, and phased milestones in his Action Plan.

Engineers Johnny and Suzy are given objectives to pilot a design thinking approach with their customer, Michael's Muffler Company. They set out to determine the customer's needs and develop an improved solution. Through this approach, Johnny and Suzy are aligned with their engineering department objectives and the overall company breakthrough goals.

They clearly understand how their daily work contributes to achieving the company's strategy. This is the real value of SGD.

My friend Don helped me hone my application of the SGD process. I first met Don when he was leading the SGD rollout for a $10 B corporation. Under his leadership and mastery of the process, impressive improvements were being realized year over year. But the company was still falling short of excellence. This shortcoming had nothing to do with Don, but two problems above him in the corporate structure.

The first problem was the company's failure to have a documented strategy. In the absence of a documented strategy, lower-level business units were forced to make assumptions. This limits the overall value of the process. It's akin to possibly solving the wrong problem. If the assumptions are incorrect, things in plain sight are often camouflaged. While SGD was returning solid improvements, without a known strategy, it's unclear if those improvements aligned with where the corporation wanted to go.

The second problem was the leaders. Those at the very top had impressive management skills. They made remarkable gains on Wall Street. While they were exceptionally effective at management, the same didn't apply for their leadership. Few would have described these top leaders as humble, authentic, or transparent. Humility and authenticity have little to do with the SGD process. But as advised earlier, a company will never achieve excellence if the top leaders don't embrace values-based leadership.

One final note on SGD, a methodology proven to help companies make the leap towards excellence. Implementing SGD does not place another administrative burden on an already over-worked staff. Instead, SGD is the tool that drives the business. People shouldn't be working on *anything* that doesn't align with the targets established by the SGD. Doing so would be equivalent to placing energy into work contrary to the company's vision.

Remember the Eisenhower decision matrix and the certainty that we spend more time on *urgent* things than on *important* things. We want to change that—we want to spend our time on important things. The SGD process helps us focus and align our efforts. And it helps ensure we spend our time on those tasks that will help us achieve the vision and move towards excellence.

6

Integrating Our Systems and Structures

SYSTEMS THINKING

Our world is made up of systems—things connected, associated, or inter-dependent, forming a complex unity. These individual *things*—let's call them *components*—along with their interactions, compose what's referred to as the *structure* of the system.

Systems thinking then is the thought process that seeks to understand the entire system through assessing how the individual components interact. It analyzes behavior by examining the whole instead of the individual parts.

We still consider the individual parts, but to understand what's control-ling behavior, we must examine the larger system. This requires we think holistically. Through this viewpoint, we're able to see the bigger picture and overcome the constraints of traditional linear thinking.

Imagine a squirrel in a forest. The squirrel is a collection of components and is itself a system. The squirrel's brain, eyes, heart, and body interact as components that make up the squirrel as a system. We could decompose these further, such as the squirrel's circulatory or respiratory system, but instead, let's go in the other direction.

The squirrel is part of a system that includes the tree in which he lives. The tree is part of a larger forest system and the forest part of an even larger ecosystem. Regardless of which system we intentionally define, interactions between the components produce the behavior of the system. Together these components and their interactions form the *structure* of the system.

Let's go back to the squirrel.

The system we'll define is the squirrel and forest where he lives. The little guy is dependent upon the trees for his food. He buries nuts throughout the fall to provide food for the winter. The forest is dependent upon the squirrel to help distribute seeds from the trees. The squirrel will not remember the hiding place of every buried nut. Those he forgets will spawn new trees to sustain the cycle of life in the forest, which is dependent upon both the tree and the squirrel.

Remove the squirrel, the tree, or the forest, and the associated interdependencies quickly become apparent. Each suffers without the presence of the other. Such is the reality of interdependencies within our companies.

The companies in which we work are systems. These organizations are themselves part of other systems, within such contexts as community, national, and global. Changes needed to move towards excellence often require alterations to these surrounding systems.

Some people may be able to complete their jobs by focusing on individual components of their work system. Those pursuing excellence cannot. They must be like systems engineers and understand how the pieces react with one another. They must understand how changing one piece affects others. They must appreciate how time, sequencing, and pace are interweaved within the whole structure.

As I stated earlier, my undergrad degree is in physics. I'm not a physicist by any means, but I enjoy the rare opportunity to apply some of this learning. Newtonian physics explains most phenomena we observe in life. For example, Lewin's Force Field Model discussed in Chapter 1 is really just Newton's Third Law of Motion: *for every action in nature there is an equal and opposite reaction.*

But not everything is explainable by classical physics. Assessing change needed to move towards excellence can sometimes challenge us to understand things beyond these laws. In some of these situations, we must defer to quantum theory.

Einstein's relativity and quantum theories reveal how we can decompose matter below the subatomic level. This decomposition continues until there are no longer any basic particles but only relationships of probabilities between the particles. When we get down to this level, *matter* isn't composed of smaller matter. It's composed of *nothing.*

If we bound our thinking to the rules of Newtonian physics, the parts fail to explain the whole because the parts are not there. The only thing that exists are probabilities of a relationship. This makes it difficult to understand the core of what something is.

Quantum physics provides the explanation. It provides the mathematics to understand the probabilities of these relationships that form the building blocks of what is.

I'm sure some may question what a discussion on mathematical relationships and probability has to do with Operational Excellence. When we're analyzing what to change, we must understand how far to break the whole down and where to draw the lines to intentionally define the "system."

Systems thinking helps us define the boundaries between what is part of the system and what is not. While we must *understand* the things that happen at this interaction level, we *manage* the issue above this level, at the system level. We manage the dynamic, not the individual pieces.

The things that we are considering here are *non-linear.*

We establish the linearity of something in relation to time, mathematics, spatial geometrics, or physics. Within the physical sense, we identify something as non-linear when outputs are independent of inputs. This non-linearity can result in small actions producing large results.

Systems thinking helps us deal with otherwise unexplainable events associated with the non-linear impact of time and physics.

For non-linear things, 1 + 1 doesn't always equal 2. We can use that to our advantage. Through applying systems thinking and principles introduced later in the book, we can achieve results where 1 + 1 equals 3. And if we're exceptionally good, and include new ways of thinking in our approach, we can develop new thoughts and ways of doing things that enable the non-linear sum of 1 + 1 to approach 11.

MANAGING COMPLEXITY

Management has an obligation to continually improve the systems and structures needed to run our companies. These are not just physical elements but include other factors such as planning and control, decision-making, and information systems used to manage the business. With a systems thinking mindset, we approach change needed to move towards excellence with a framework that accounts for the inherent complexities, contradictory natures, and interdependencies.

Now we need to quickly examine the word *complex*. We sometimes casually interchange complex and complicated, but they're different concepts, especially with respect to systems. In simple words, complicated systems are rich in *detail* and complex systems are rich in *structure*.

Systems with only a few components and few interdependencies may be complicated but are not complex. Complex systems are full of interdependencies. Complexity is the resulting product from many interacting and diverse parts. These parts act in a non-linear fashion that can't be reduced to a simple computation to predict future outcomes.

For the simplest of examples, let's consider a maze or labyrinth to be complicated and a multi-level series of interworking gears to be complex. In most cases, the change we're seeking as we move towards excellence will be complex. Understanding and accounting for this complexity in an environment of continual change requires a different kind of thinking. And not one that we normally use.

There are two different processes for how we assess information to understand.

The first way we process information is through analysis. This process breaks down the whole into its individual parts and components. We gain a better understanding of the whole through analyzing the smaller parts. The second way is through synthesis. This is the opposite process by which we combine separate components to form the whole. Synthesis is a higher process that creates something new.

Analysis spawns analytical thinking while synthesis leads to systems thinking. Both are necessary on our journey to excellence, but as indicated in Figure 6.1, they pursue different paths to get there.

Let's return to our maze and gears. Analysis is the typical process applied to solve complicated problems, like our maze. The solution here requires *analysis* to break down the individual parts that present potential solutions for the escape path. But to understand how the gears work together to form the complex unity, we need to understand each one on its own, its interdependencies to the other gears, and how it contributes to the larger system. Solving complex problems such as this requires *synthesis*.

Managers are trained to solve complicated problems using analysis. They are not trained to solve complex problems using synthesis. This shouldn't surprise us. Many companies have numerous roles with Analyst in the title. I know of none with Synthesist as a title. I typed *Analyst* as a key word into a popular job search engine, and it returned 120,000 advertised jobs. *Synthesist* returned none.

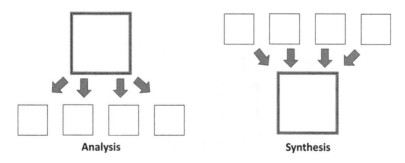

Analysis   **Synthesis**

FIGURE 6.1

Analysis versus synthesis.

Outside of systems theory classes, there's no real training path for complex problems. The result is that we analyze complex problems and try to solve them in a linear manner. That won't achieve the needed solutions. Complex problems require a systems approach and one that considers the interdependencies and uses synthesis to help arrive at the solution. This reality needs our attention.

Now, I want to pivot slightly and introduce a related subject before leaving this concept.

Analysis and synthesis are thought processes we apply to deal with data, challenges, and issues in our work routine. Sub-optimization is the product of one of those issues. And it's a self-induced problem that presents itself repeatedly in companies stalled in average performance.

Sub-optimization comes about through errors in execution. It occurs when we focus improvements on one component of a system and ignore the effect on other components, as indicated in Figure 6.2. Interdependencies are in play here. While the focused component may realize improvements, the overall net result is degraded system performance. Shifting our thoughts to think in terms of the system can help us avoid this common trap.

Increasing pressures and resource constraints require that we employ a systems approach to manage the bigger picture. When doing so, we must be cautious against prioritizing projects based only on the fact that their leaders have more political influence or are more articulate than others. What is best for these persuasive leaders may not be what is best for the business.

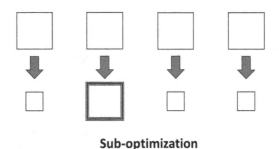

Sub-optimization

FIGURE 6.2

Sub-optimization.

The squeaky wheel isn't always the one that needs the most grease. And it shouldn't be the only one that gets greased. Moving towards excellence requires that we consider the larger system and provide an optimized solution that returns the greatest overall result.

RISK AND OPPORTUNITY THINKING

I faced a common risk decision on my way to the office this morning.

Driving on the freeway at 70 mph, I noticed a large block of wood in my lane 200 ft ahead. I would be on it within two seconds. *Observing* the wood set my brain into an OODA cycle. I *oriented* to the environment and noted two motorcycles to the left, a semi-truck to the right, and a car 100 ft behind. I ruled out changing lanes or applying the breaks and *decided* to drive over the obstacle. I *acted* and my truck's tires crushed the wood. The ensuing force sprayed debris that landed on the car following too closely behind. I then *observed* no apparent harm and we each continued on our way.

We all employ a certain level of risk-based thinking within our daily routines. We choose to, or not to, cross the road before the walk sign signals us. We choose to drive at the speed limit or not. We order the steak and loaded baked potato or the salad and fish. We assess how many multiples of our salary to carry in life insurance. And we decide whether or not to leave the puppy in the house while we run to the market.

Unfortunately, we all now have a new appreciation for risk thanks to the pandemic. As the situation subsides and we put more time between us and the event, we'll soon start changing our behavior based upon the reduced risk. We continually conduct mental assessments and act upon our risk-based decisions. Doing so is an inherent part of being human. And most of us are good at this. Not to be Darwinian, but those of us who aren't are here in more of a temporary nature.

When we decide to walk across the street in traffic, we're assuming risk. As soon as we reach the other side, the risk is retired, unless we get a ticket for jaywalking. We seldom retire business risks so quickly. We typically manage this process through formal documented procedures. We can get additional help through software systems that help us identify, track, and mitigate risks. But much more important than any tool is the thought process and mindset used to manage risks and exploit opportunities.

In 2015, ISO released an update to the quality management standard used by more than one million companies. With this revision, ISO placed intentional emphasis on addressing risks and opportunities. I believe the standard writers realized failure to manage risk doesn't just impede a company from conforming behavior, but it can degrade them below even average performance.

Risk is the relative degree that we're exposed to harm or an undesired condition. It cannot be managed in silos, separated from the larger systems and structures. But this is often the approach taken across our companies. Risk presented to a subordinate element inherently applies to the entire organization.

Considering this truth, I'm amazed how many companies fail to manage risk at the enterprise level. Responsibility for managing the risk may still rest with the cognizant function most exposed to the risk, or that first identified the risk, but awareness must be shared up the chain.

Many internal factors work against efforts to improve our risk management. The culture can resist our effort to manage risk at the enterprise level, driven by issues traced back to trust, transparency, and accountability. And something we'll discuss in the final chapter, "structural secrecy" precludes people from sharing up the chain information required by top management. The result is sub-optimization of risk. And it causes significant jeopardy to our companies.

Not managing risks and opportunities at the enterprise level results in a sub-optimal solution that fails to account for interdependencies within the system. In addition, doing so likely results in missed opportunities to capitalize upon that which could help us on our journey to excellence.

The Competing Values Framework (CVF) can help us here. I've already introduced several applications of the CVF and how it can adjust our thinking as we move towards excellence. As I mentioned before, many other researchers have expanded the CVF applications since introduced by Rohrbaugh and Quinn. My addition uses the framework to balance the paradox of managing organizational risks and opportunities.

Risks and opportunities exist along the same spectrum. But different thought processes are needed to identify and mitigate risks than those needed to identify and capitalize on opportunities.

The base framework identifies those leadership traits, value drivers, and theories of effectiveness most applicable to the four different culture types. Organizations seek out leaders with characteristics identified by the leadership traits for their cultural focus. The value drivers represent those elements perceived as important, and the theory of effectiveness frames the mechanics for how the business is managed.

As related by Figure 6.3, opportunity management resides in the *create* quadrant while risk management is in the *control* quadrant. When seeking to exploit opportunities, we employ those leadership traits, value drivers, and theories of effectiveness from the upper right quadrant, which vary dramatically from the lower left. Neither characteristics are right or wrong on their own, but each can be ineffective if employed at the wrong time and with the wrong mindset.

Many companies struggle to manage opportunities. They under-value this process. This can result in allowing a potential competitive advantage to slip through our fingers. Companies sometimes depart from the

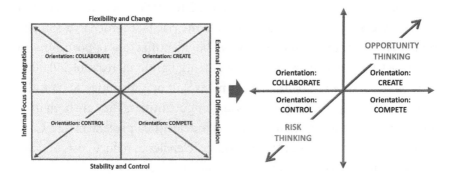

FIGURE 6.3

CVF risks and opportunities. (Adapted with permission from *Diagnosing and Changing Organizational Culture.*)

American spirit that drives us to be our best. Once we achieve a certain level of success, we may become hyper-conservative when assessing risks and opportunities. Doing so results in a failure to take advantage of potential competitive advantages.

Within competitive sports, great measures are taken to exploit even the smallest competitive advantage. Mature businesses seldom pursue such bold actions. Well, some companies embrace this bold behavior. And these are the ones that attain excellence.

Some of this behavior traces to our inherent negativity bias. We fail to recognize goodness with the same level of clarity as we do that which is negative. Psychologists tell us this is innate. While the full explanation is complicated, we do it as a survival mechanism traced to our need to prioritize behavior against threats.

Another reason could be our status quo bias, explained by loss aversion theory. We have a strong tendency to prefer avoiding losses over acquiring gains. To fully exploit the opportunities available to our business, we must start to disconfirm these thoughts and biases.

Again, new ways of thinking will be required on our journey to excellence.

Imagine a manufacturer secures a purchase order of $500,000 for 5,000 widgets. To simplify this, let's assume the work was estimated with a cost of goods sold (COGS) of $80 per unit, returning a potential profit of $100,000. Before starting the work, the Production Manager records a risk of COGS increasing to $90 per unit. The risk is recorded as a $50,000 potential profit reduction. Similarly, he identifies an opportunity to decrease COGS to $70 per unit and a potential profit increase of $50,000.

Actions are taken to reduce costs and exploit opportunities. Such is the typical approach of managing risks and opportunities. They are both usually approached using management characteristics present in the CVF lower left *control* quadrant. We seek out efficiencies to reduce costs and are satisfied with something that is often much less than optimal.

But what if we approached this differently? What if we incorporated thinking from the CVF upper right *create* quadrant to assess new ways to create breakthrough opportunities?

We could employ different thoughts to identify opportunities to reduce COGS to $50 per unit, returning a potential profit of $250,000. While it may not be possible, challenging ourselves to be uncomfortable and think of new ways to approach the problem can return results never before envisioned. This is the essence of real opportunity management.

I don't want to get too deep into this as we'll further explore this in later chapters. But the "cost plus view of price" results in a failure to exploit opportunities to reduce costs. When profit remains our driving factor and fixed as a near constant, management remains happy. They remain blinded from opportunities to further reduce costs and realize greater sustainable profits.

OUR CHANGING ORGANIZATIONAL CONSTRUCT

From a systems standpoint, the most important structure of our companies, and the one which drives the most interdependencies, is the actual construct of the organization. Across our companies, these base structures are transforming. And the pace of this transformation is increasing.

Common structure orientations include functional, product, geographical, and customer. There are blends of others, such as strategy and environment. But the functional structure with a hierarchical orientation remains dominant in many of our companies, even when it no longer aligns to current needs. Such functional structures often end up driving a constraining internal focus.

Forward leading companies seeking to move beyond average recognize the incompatibility of top-down hierarchical structures with the agility required in today's marketspace. The quantity of information to be processed, education, and different values and beliefs of a younger work force are just some of the paradigms challenging the continued efficacy of this structure.

Our new organizational dynamics, to include the active use of teams, work against the basic tenants of the hierarchical organization. And as people seek empowerment and to actively participate in the decision-making process, these structures become even more problematic.

In the hierarchical organization, the structure itself provides the basis for formal authority. The decision-making process here is almost always unilateral.

Under a legacy hierarchical structure, senior management issue directives, middle management make tactical decisions and assign tasks, and supervisors ensure front-line workers follow directions. Few companies would admit to this as their construct. Many believe they operate an agile learning organization with an innovative, creative, and empowered workforce. But this is another concept hijacked by reality.

These legacy constructs no longer meet our needs. They're based upon a classical management structure that assumes a servant manager–worker relation, but where the worker serves the manager. The structure limits empowerment and engagement. And it remains overly dependent upon supervision and the use of metrics tied to individual employee performance.

Mid-size and larger companies that don't cling to a rigid top-down structure are the exception. The realm needed to move towards excellence and more resilience has little in common with these legacy structures.

To implement this movement, senior management must transcend beyond merely issuing directives. Senior leaders must establish a clear purpose for the company, with documented core values and beliefs that drive behavior and challenge the organization to achieve breakthrough goals. Middle management must move beyond minor decisions and task assignment. They need to assume the role of removing barriers and enabling the workforce. And front-line workers no longer focus on merely doing what they're told. Instead, they help identify problems and generate ideas for improvement.

Much of this current issue is about to be obviated. It will soon be overcome by beliefs of a changing workforce and new realities of a post-pandemic world. Even prior to the pandemic, this demographic shift began changing our definition of work. What the word meant to someone 30 years ago bears little resemblance to where we're headed. While many companies previously resisted remote work, our recent events have shattered those paradigms. Companies that don't figure out how to optimize remote work will be left behind by our new world.

While our new work environment will be different, the people moving into our workforce are also different. Much has been written about these "digital natives" and their different values and beliefs. They view the work life balance thing through a different lens. They have different expectations for feedback and a larger concern for the interdependency of their work to the environment. They're also good people, just like those before them and those who will come after them.

Millennials now make up the largest demographic of working-age employees. The different experiences they grew up with provided them different beliefs and ways of thinking. And just behind Millennials are Gen Z, the largest generation in the United States with about 90 million people.

I sometimes hear companies refer to our current workforce changes as a problem. The best companies don't have a Millennial problem and aren't seeking a solution. They don't need a solution because they don't view a younger workforce as a problem. They recognize this isn't some new issue to be solved.

The continual re-introduction of younger workers with different values and beliefs has been the recurring state of business since the first industrial revolution. In 1899, Elbert Hubbard penned *A Message to Garcia* and wrote about the frustration of business owners over young clerk's "half-hearted work" ethic. The generation Hubbard complained about would be our great-great-grandparents now.

Some things, it seems, never change.

The best companies don't have a Millennial problem because they understand these Millennials, and behind them Gen Z, are people. And leaders, first and foremost, are in the business of people. We embrace what each person brings to the situation and work with them so that together we can move closer to excellence.

FRAGILE versus ROBUST

The coronavirus pandemic exposed many weaknesses in our systems and structures. Some we know about already. More are yet to be identified.

Forthcoming works by other authors will assess the global, national, and local systems that let us down. My focus here are the ones within our companies. Few could argue these systems and structures weren't more fragile than we previously realized.

Our companies became over-leveraged in our new connected world. This applied to areas beyond finances and impacted many of our internal systems and structures. We maybe took some things too far, and we became exposed. The continual pursuit of lower costs through global sourcing led to intolerable vulnerabilities. Our supply chains were not only over-leveraged, but we found that they lacked diversification necessary to withstand geo-economic instabilities.

The concluding chapter will fully analyze the different approaches companies take with respect to price, cost, and value. In that discussion, we'll see how some of the most forward-leaning companies emphasized cost reductions to the point that they jeopardized diversification and long-term sustainability. Such actions have proven to increase fragility in a now uncertain world.

The word *fragile* is an important word. The dictionary tells us that it's something easily broken or damaged. We've certainly witnessed a great deal of that fragility lately.

It's interesting to note that John Krafcik, who coined the term Lean, considered a company's systems, and therefore the companies themselves, to range from fragile to robust. He introduced new terms for this range, defining them from *lean* to *buffered*. Those maintaining minimum inventories and just-in-time delivery to the point of need are *lean*. They do so at higher risk but with far greater opportunity for cost savings. Those with redundant systems and high inventory levels are *buffered* against disruption. These buffered systems induce less risk but also provide far less opportunities for cost savings.

As the coronavirus pandemic unfolded, our supply chains became one of the first systems exposed. We quickly became aware of the extent that our logistics were over-extended. Then the problem got worse. Some companies and commodities experienced a lagging effect and are just now starting to realize the full impact.

Some blame the philosophies of Lean. I don't. Within our American businesses, Lean has never been fully embraced. One Lean concept that has been embraced by many though is the practice of driving costs down through a global-sourcing strategy and reduced inventories. This strategy has been vigorously expanded since the mid-1990s. And therein lies the problem.

Failing to diversify the supply chain with an ever-increasing desire to source material with the lowest cost, regardless of location and sustained availability, creates fragility within even the best companies. Nearly a decade ago, it happened to Toyota, the very source of ideas behind Toyota Production System (TPS) and Lean.

A March 2011 earthquake exposed weaknesses in Toyota's supply chain management. The earthquake and resulting tsunami crushed Toyota's supply chain, causing widespread part shortages for weeks. The impact to Toyota's profits was devastating.

The most robust systems and structures are ones that are diversified. They are not overly dependent upon any one element. When designing our systems and structures, care must be taken to design out single points of failure. We must design them to be *robust.* The lessons from the pandemic will be learned and studied for some time. Indeed, there is so much more to be learned in the months and years ahead.

I've been advocating for years that Lean doesn't have to be an absolute. And I've been proposing that we need to view our world through a different lens; a lens that doesn't require an all or nothing approach. The CVF provides us a tool and thought process to embrace those Lean ideas which strengthen our systems and structures. And it guides us to ignore those which make them more fragile. Lean purists would resist such a partial approach. But the best leaders know we are responsible for how we choose to implement our systems and structures.

As we plan our strategies to move our companies forward, we can use the Strategic Goal Deployment (SGD) process to help us. We can use SGD to strategize robustness into our supply chains and other internal systems and structures with specific action plans that drive us towards achieving something better than what we had before.

We'll return to this idea of *fragile*, and its opposite of *antifragile*, when we discuss Black Swans in the next chapter. In this current discussion, I sought only to emphasize that we must make our systems and structures more robust. The ensuing discussion will assess the new marketspaces these systems and structures must integrate within to help make our companies more resilient.

7

Understanding Our Marketspace

Organizational design theorists and practitioners agree the most critical element to a company's success is culture. Culture is the inward element that defines how things get done around here. It follows the marketspace is the outward element that establishes *where* things get done and directly influences *why* they get done.

But the marketspace is much more than simply the place where we sell goods and services. It encompasses elements across the expanded industry space, including the competitive dynamics, the types of solutions offered in that market, the actions of influential players, and the driving forces that shape the space. Our journey to excellence requires we be more than just aware of our marketspace. We must be actively engaged with an intentional plan.

The marketspace doesn't create anything. It processes information and then reflects it back to us. We respond with our continually improved products and services. The marketspace will dictate business behavior of the future, as it has done in the past. And the marketspace is changing—changing fast and with great magnitude. Our companies must be prepared to change with an equivalent response.

MARKET LIFE CYCLES AND LEADERSHIP

As businesses mature, the culture inherently adjusts. These cultural changes follow a predictable pattern. The pattern for most companies matures from an early external focus on flexibility and discretion to eventually become more internally focused on structure and integration. Predicting and responding to this pattern is key to planning a construct that embraces agility while creating the structure needed for disciplined and scaled growth.

As the business continues to mature and the culture moves through this progression, people will begin to have new experiences that will form new beliefs. These will drive cultural changes. Leaders recognize this and take action to reinforce desired behavior by creating and strengthening desired experiences as the company grows and matures.

In the wonderful book *The First 90 Days*, Michael Watkins introduced a heuristic to help identify organizational life cycles. Watkins described the life cycles companies progress through as *start-up, turnaround, accelerated growth, realignment,* and *sustaining success.* I first learned of this model 15 years ago while preparing for a senior management role. I've been applying it ever since.

Expanding on Watkins' ideas, a given company operates in an overall life cycle stage while its functional elements and business units may be in different stages. A high-volume factory may have mature processes and be optimized for Lean manufacturing initiatives. The same factory may lack adequate Human Resources support and be in a turnaround relative to employee relations. Recognizing these stages provides insight when trying to affect change necessary to achieve excellence.

Watkins' work provides us a model to help assess the company and make assumptions about prevailing behaviors within that life cycle. The Competing Values Framework provides another.

Organizations evolve predictably over time. And their cultures follow a predictable pattern. The CVF demonstrates how new companies are dominated by the *create* quadrant in their early years. Through their middle years, they evolve to a culture dominated by the *collaborate* quadrant. Eventually, most mature to a culture dominated by the *compete* or *control* quadrants, dependent upon their marketspace and product portfolio.

Using CVF applications discussed to this point, we can improve our understanding of life cycle management by combining the CVF with concepts from Watkins' model. With this hybrid approach, we can see

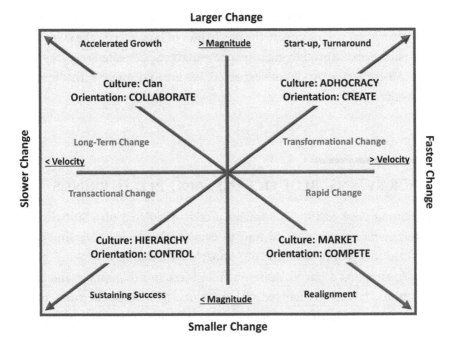

FIGURE 7.1

CVF and organizational life cycles. (Adapted with permission from *Diagnosing and Changing Organizational Culture.*)

how a particular life cycle affects the desired culture and orientation. We can also see the type of change expected to be dominant by identifying the relative magnitude and velocity of that change, as represented in Figure 7.1.

Let's consider an application for a company seeking to break into new markets. We previously reviewed how breakthrough goals can challenge an organization to performance never before believed possible. Entering new markets, introducing new products, or adopting a different business model will each require us to think differently. Each of these indicates transformational change.

The market leadership needed to succeed here resides in the CVF upper right quadrant. When taking this bold path, the company's orientation may resemble that of a start-up or turnaround. The leadership traits and values needed may differ dramatically from that normally embraced across the organization. And the theory of effectiveness informs us that vision and innovation will dominate the mechanics of how we run the show.

Pursuing breakthrough goals in a new marketspace often requires bold and decisive action. And that's expected. We are told, after all, that fortune favors the bold.

BLACK SWANS, BLUE OCEANS, AND RED HERRINGS

A warning prior to the 2008 financial crisis predicted instability in risk management methods could lead to catastrophic events. Nassim Taleb provided this prophecy in his 2007 book, *The Black Swan*.

Taleb supplied a narrative on our blindness to randomness and large deviations. His ideas changed our thoughts, to include the most influential thinkers, on this concept of random events and their impact. *The Black Swan* brings new context to unknown unknowns. Taleb didn't try to get us to predict Black Swan events but to build robustness within our systems and structures to be able to withstand such events.

As the coronavirus became a pandemic, many claimed it to be a Black Swan event. Taleb himself was irritated with that analogy, stating the pandemic was not a Black Swan because we knew about the potential for such a crisis. He even predicted it 13 years earlier in his book when he wrote, "I see risks of a very strange acute virus spreading throughout the planet."

Taleb is right that we knew about it. The pandemic wasn't an unknown unknown. There were many predictions, to include the generic one Bill Gates provided in a 2015 TED Talk. Some were much more specific. A 2007 paper in *Clinical Microbiology Reviews* provided an ominous warning. While it's now moot, the subject paper stated, "The presence of a large reservoir of SARS-CoV-like viruses in horseshoe bats, together with the culture of eating exotic mammals in southern China, is a time bomb."

Some argue the resulting impact makes the pandemic a Black Swan. That's a hard point to justify when so many identified the risk as a known. We just failed to plan. Five years after *The Black Swan*, Taleb authored another thought-provoker with his book *Antifragile*. He expanded his analysis of "uncertainty, probability, human error, risk, and decision-making in a world we don't understand." He also provided what he described as the "antidote to Black Swans" as that which is *antifragile*.

In Chapter 6, we examined the concept of fragile and how many of our systems and structures proved to be fragile in the wake of the coronavirus. We also discussed the spectrum from fragile to robust that our companies operate within. And we discussed that certain aspects of Lean, as applied by some companies, exposed our fragility, especially within our extended supply chains.

In *Antifragile*, Taleb offers a new end to that spectrum so that it ranges from *fragile* to *robust* to *antifragile*. He defines antifragile as the opposite of fragile and something that is beyond resilience and robustness. Taleb explains that something which is resilient resists shock and stays the same, but an entity that is antifragile gets stronger.

As the coronavirus expanded its grip, it soon became obvious that our companies fit into one of three categories as defined by these new definitions, with representative examples indicated below:

Fragile	Travel, hospitality, luxury goods, fine dining
Robust	Business to business, defense contractors, healthcare
Antifragile	Delivery services, video-conferencing tools, remote-based work

Early in the first week of April 2020, one of America's largest manufacturers recognized the need for immediate planning for a new marketspace. In a letter to all employees, Boeing Chief Executive Dave Calhoun wrote, "When the world emerges from the pandemic, the size of the commercial market and the types of products and services our customers want and need will likely be different."

Throughout this book, we've been discussing new applications of proven tools we can use to help us achieve excellence. But we'll need more than just new tools. We will need new ways of thinking. And we will need to develop new strategies. The world has changed. We will need these new strategies that allow us to view our situation from a different perspective.

In *Blue Ocean Strategy*, Chan Kim and Renée Mauborgne discuss a corporate strategy to move beyond choosing between differentiation and low cost to creating a "Blue Ocean," pursuing *both* differentiation *and* low cost simultaneously. Although the authors don't identify it as such, this is the essence of both/and thinking and the CVF.

This way of thinking isn't possible unless we approach the problem from a systems perspective. Without a systems approach, we may not be aware of other choices and resign to a position where we're forced to choose one or the other. But both choices are often possible. We just need a different perspective.

We typically conduct a SWOT analysis to help identify internal and external factors that could affect performance. The analysis looks at how the organization fits into our current reality. But a SWOT analysis also provides insight to the *needs* and *ideas* we'll need to move towards excellence.

We don't typically conduct a SWOT with the intent of identifying change. Rather, the independent task of conducting a SWOT to assess business posture produces artifacts that serve as indicators of potential change facing the organization, the *needs* and *ideas* that will result in change.

Kim and Mauborgne put forth a SWOT variant combined with the *start, stop, and continue* tool used to improve individual leader behavior. They refer to their tool as the *Four Actions Framework* and as the cornerstone of a strategy intended to identify new marketspaces.

Their framework seeks to identify actions a company needs to eliminate, reduce, create, and improve to adjust the business focus to capitalize in markets without competition. Like a SWOT analysis, leaders don't set out using this to identify change. But artifacts provided from the framework predict change about to be imposed on, or sought by, the organization.

Kim and Mauborgne's book is a landmark effort. Most executives and entrepreneurs now take for granted the ideas of the *Blue Ocean* analogy. In this regard, we can argue the strategy as a relative business truth. As we continue this journey towards excellence in our new environment, we must explore these Blue Oceans as part of our growth strategy focused on both *needs* and *ideas*.

Near opposite of the Blue Ocean is the red herring. Many of us recognize a red herring as the rough draft of a company's prospectus that includes a description of the business plan, financial condition, strategy, and management details. That is not fish we're concerned with here.

I'm referring to the red herring of the literary world, something that intentionally misleads us from a more important issue and results in drawing a false conclusion.

In business, and in life, how we get results matter. It matters a lot. Ethics are not relative. And the ends should never be used to justify the means, especially if those means end up harming others. The discussion here is on businesses that sometimes portray themselves to be something they are not. In the worst cases, these become more than just deceitful behavior. And unfortunately, there are many examples.

Social media companies have been known to create fake accounts to enhance their marketing platforms. Software application providers are notorious for aggressively spamming our email. And others use deceitful methods to obtain phone numbers then try to get us to download unwanted applications.

In Chapter 12, we'll discuss analytics and the growing need for companies to develop *prescriptive analytics*. Using prescriptive analytics, we seek to control, manipulate, and improve our processes and systems so that we can improve the value of the product provided to the customer. For most industries, this doesn't create any sort of ethical dilemma. But in the social media arena, we must acknowledge that the advertisers have become the customers and we as the users have become the product. This industry's growing ability to influence, control, and manipulate our lives is one of significant concern, and although it is a red herring, it is also a problem beyond the scope of this book.

But perpetrators here aren't limited to social media and application providers. Some well-known multi-billion-dollar companies have employed tactics to trick and deceive customers. We've seen scandals across most every industry. Possibly the worst of these are the actions of Wells Fargo and its practice of creating millions of fraudulent accounts that recently resulted in a $3 B civil penalty.

The concern isn't limited to these deceitful practices or even those that operate within the margins. As competition increases in our new global marketspace, it appears certain companies will do anything to succeed. Some even argue our classical management structure and focus on the shareholder drives companies towards misrepresentation, deception, and other deceitful practices. We'll explore that idea further in Chapter 11 when we discuss the purpose of business.

We all know some people that liberally embellish their qualifications. These range from self-identification on social media as a "thought leader" to more harmful methods of claiming unearned credentials to secure unknowing clients. And organizationally, companies present similar façades when they profess to have leading strategies in the newest thoughts and ideas. When something is perceived to be a positive quality, it is often quickly claimed, even if it isn't possessed.

Some companies embrace the principles of Lean and Six Sigma as part of their core business models. Others haven't embraced the concepts but still use them as a tagline and claimed differentiator. Some reading this book may connect the dots and make a genuine effort to move their companies towards true business transformation and Operational Excellence. And others will continue to merely claim excellence and use it within their taglines and functional titles.

Both are okay, I guess, even the ones that are only a façade. But the ones genuinely pursuing excellence will be the only ones positioned to succeed with the changes coming to our marketspaces.

QUALITY 4.0

The fourth industrial revolution is upon us. The introduction of mechanization, steam power, and the weaving loom brought about the first revolution 250 years ago. Electrical energy, mass production, and the assembly line led the second revolution 100 years later. Just 50 years ago, automation, computers, and electronics signaled the third revolution. And now we're embarking on the fourth revolution, led by the

Internet of Things, cyber-physical systems, artificial intelligence, and networks.

Ten years ago, a group of German political, business, and academic leaders coined the term for this latest revolution as *Industry 4.0*. Others embraced the idea to the point that it became a global movement of increasing momentum. Technological advancements in the areas of data, analytics, and connectivity are driving real paradigm shifts to the way we run our businesses.

These transformational changes started to induce major cultural changes that required our attention. Then a pandemic changed the course of history, and with it, the trajectory of this latest movement.

But regardless, our workforce make-up and constructs are changing. The leadership needed to move our companies forward is changing. And our approach to how we innovate, secure materials, measure performance, and ensure quality are all also changing. These changes are transforming how we manage our companies and lead to what many began branding as *Quality 4.0*, a derivative of Industry 4.0.

While there are different theories, most agree the base components that comprise this Quality 4.0 framework focus on 12 distinct attributes, as represented below:

Data	Collaboration	Management systems
Analytics	Scalability	Competency
Connectivity	Compliance	Leadership
Application development	Culture	Customer intimacy

But I'm not completely buying this, yet. Maybe I'm not willing to be an early adopter for the latest fad. Or more accurately, it's because I see a strong correlation between the principles discussed in this book and those of Quality 4.0.

Any resistance I have isn't due to any unwillingness to accept change. Rather, as I have discussed throughout this work, I believe there's a different approach based upon fundamental leadership and management practices that provide us the surest path to achieving higher performance in our new world.

We must always balance the value offered by better tools and systems against the desire to improve how we do things. The Quality profession, in general, suffers from a lack of understanding of its larger role at the higher levels. Polls and surveys consistently reveal a lack of senior leadership understanding of the importance of quality. Historically, less than 15 percent of executives typically believe that quality is a priority for top management.

The result of this reality is the maturity of quality systems and tools often lag other internal systems. The effect is a Quality organization that is often still trying to solve yesterday's problems. We need to make sure we don't become distracted by the next shiny object as we move our Quality organizations forward towards this desired state of excellence.

We need to temper our fascination with the latest approach with the recognition that our priority should always be on people, ideas, and then tools, and in that order.

But eventually, this digital transformation will be a path that all will need to embrace. As we make progress towards achieving system autonomy, we can reduce the time allocated to execution and instead provide an increased focus on improvement and innovation. This is the common path between Quality 4.0 and Operational Excellence.

Part III

Things We Do See

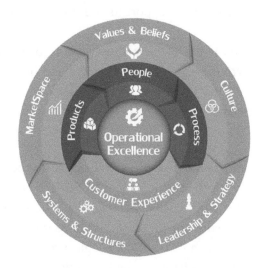

I don't watch much TV, but I do enjoy Marcus Lemonis' show, *The Profit*. His "three P mantra" is founded on the principle that business success is focused on *people*, *process*, and *product*.

The mantra of "people, process, and product" is catchy. But it's also a little misleading. Limiting our focus to these will always fall short if we don't address the surrounding interdependencies. As we're about to discuss, I'm also a strong believer in the importance of people, process, and product. But there's more to this equation that we must consider.

Having the right people is critical. That's a given. But to optimize contributions from the people, we must first ensure they're aligned with the organization in their values and beliefs. If they're not, no amount of coaching or encouraging will achieve the sought-after results.

A weak correlation between a company and employee value systems creates problems. People will struggle if there isn't alignment between the organization and their values and beliefs. They will struggle because people won't embrace what they don't value. This will create problems with their commitment. And if they aren't committed, we won't be able to move towards excellence.

Having the right processes is also paramount to success. But these processes are defined by, and operate within, the systems and structures of the business. We can develop a perfect process, but if the surrounding systems and structures don't support its use, the process won't add the needed value.

Any attempt to fix issues in the people, process, or products without addressing the surrounding culture, the values and beliefs, the systems and structures, and the leadership and strategy will preclude us from becoming operationally excellent.

Back to *The Profit*.

When Marcus chooses not to make a deal, he claims the most common reason is an issue with the *people*. But when he does make a deal and it doesn't succeed, I believe it's usually due to deeper issues within the values and beliefs or systems and structures. What doesn't prevent him from succeeding once making a deal are the people, processes, and products, which he often changes under his going-in position of being "100 percent in charge."

That works for a television show. But we don't run our companies that way. Or at least we don't if we're pursuing excellence.

8

Engaging Our People

Leaders are in the people business. They incur a tremendous responsibility to nurture the personal development and professional growth of employees. Anyone who doesn't believe that stopped reading this book long ago.

Most of this book discusses thoughts and ideas focused on company leaders. This chapter departs from that pattern with a perspective that focuses on the people within our companies.

THE BUSINESS OF PEOPLE

We people are sentient beings full of feelings and emotions. And we sometimes confuse feelings with emotions. While we often interchange these terms, they have important distinctions to clarify.

Feelings are physical sensations or perceptions gained through the sense of touch or the general sensibility of the body. They're the internal response our body provides to external stimuli. Emotions relate our mental inference stemming from psychological or physiological signals or body changes. They're a state of changing consciousness. In this regard, emotions are instinctive and not tied to reasoning or knowledge.

I'm under no illusion that all readers will be comfortable and agree with this ensuing conversation. If I'm going to lose some of the more hardened leaders, this is the place.

The change we'll be inviting in our pursuit of excellence creates emotional responses. The emotional presence is so dominant that we classify change as an affective event, meaning it is emotion laden and creates emotional responses. When we lead people through this environment towards excellence, we must connect with them with both our heart and our mind.

I previously failed to grasp this. I was a Marine and believed that being direct, without emotion, was the most effective leadership style. I was wrong.

I'm still direct, but I now understand that my connection was limited to the mind. I was more than not connecting with the heart; I was ignoring it completely. My approach created a blind spot in my leadership. But I eventually learned through some gifted instruction under Dr. Ken Blanchard, and experience, that success in our challenging environment of continual change requires emotional awareness. I learned to understand and appreciate the emotions of those I lead towards excellence.

One could argue with a certain degree of credibility that corporations are intentionally designed to be emotionally barren. Somehow, managers have been led to believe we must check our emotions at the door. When we do so, it's the organization that loses. Such an environment results in leaving behind much of our ability to add value. We may still make positive contributions but will do so with less creativity, ideas, and solutions than we could if not divorced from our emotional thoughts.

For those companies determined to pursue excellence, change and the emotion it creates will be constant. Knowing this, we shouldn't construct our work environs as places absent of emotions and feelings. When we do make this intentional effort to exclude emotions, or even the subliminal effort to ignore them, undesired events can exasperate an already difficult situation.

Emotions are human nature. To deny them is to deny being human. Most of us work from eight to ten hours a day in our companies and will do so for at least 40 years. We shouldn't try to deny our true selves for what amounts to such a large portion of our life. In those companies that get it, that outperform their competitors, leaders are encouraged to consider the entire system, to include the congruence of daily operations and emotions.

Whether we work in a traditional construct or a remote work environment, the importance of emotions remains consistent. As we transitioned to remote work during the pandemic, the number of meetings filling the day gradually increased. Small issues and quick planning events previously handled through passing hall talk now needed to be coordinated through scheduled web meetings. The absence of a human connection soon became apparent. I addressed this by dedicating the first ten minutes of web meetings to just talking. We spent that valuable time reconnecting with one another as people.

A common criticism I've received over the latter part of my career is that I wear my heart on my sleeve. I now find myself wishing more people would do the same.

ENGAGEMENT

The very definition of work is changing. That being said, some of us work at a job we love. We work with great people in a company that maintains a social conscience and where our values and beliefs align. Our work gives us a sense of purpose. We look forward to work and the ability to grow emotionally, spiritually, and mentally.

Those of us who work in such an environment are fortunate.

But we need to be honest here. We all don't have this same experience. Gallup tells us there are two unhappy employees for every one that is happy. Prior to the pandemic, more than a third of companies historically identified engagement as their number one business challenge. I believe it's safe to say at this point, no one really knows how our new environment is going to affect engagement. But I'm willing to bet its importance will at least remain, if not significantly increase.

Those of us who don't work in a positive environment find work to be something of lesser value than what it should be. Remember, people won't embrace what they don't value. If people don't value and feel a sense of belonging to their work, it's only a matter of time until an emotional detachment sets in. Such an environment acts as a major hindrance towards achieving excellence.

Back when I was in college, I worked in a window manufacturing plant. It's the only time I've been fired. This was a miserable job. The supervisors roamed the plant like prison guards, poised to deliver punishment for any perceived violation. Each day concluded with a daily stampede to the time clock. I was young but still knew enough to challenge the way things were being done. Eventually, I was fired. I was okay with that outcome.

After college, I went into the Marine Corps and had the opportunity to do some amazing things. I got to be a Marine and to lead Marines. And I got to see the world. Anytime friends or family questioned how long I was going to stay in the service, I always replied, "When it stops being fun."

It stopped being fun for me 15 years into my service, so I resigned my commission. I kept my promise and look back on each day with pride. I can do so because I held true to myself. No person or action was to blame; I just lost my emotional commitment. I couldn't change my perspective of what my life had become, so I changed my environment.

Throughout my career, I've become familiar with a certain minority set of people that are unhappy in their environment. This group equates to those Gallup classifies as "actively disengaged." There's a much larger group that Gallup classifies as "not engaged." Collectively, these two groups are claimed to make up 70 percent of the typical US workforce. That's amazing if we think about it.

I often wonder what keeps people in a place where they've become unhappy. I realize some are tied to a future pension, the proverbial golden handcuffs. But I struggle with that notion. Life is too short to remain in a perennial state of unhappiness. I recognize geo-economic ties and responsibilities for supporting a family, but this situation requires some reflection. If someone isn't happy in their position, they should either change their perspective or change their environment.

This discussion depends on our interpretation of perspective and perception, which are different ideas that impact engagement and are worthy of quick clarification.

Perspective is the place from where we look at things. It's how we see things from our position. If we're looking down from an airplane, we have an aerial perspective. A boss inherently has a different way of looking at a situation than an employee. Perception comprises our deductions from our perspective.

It's the perception of our reality that governs our perspective towards life.

To be effective, leaders must try to understand the perceptions of those under their charge to better appreciate the perspective of those they lead.

Many of us see things differently, to include our organizations and our role within them. The good news is that perspective isn't permanent. The only thing holding us back from changing our perspective is ourselves. The main attributes involved here are judgment, moral courage, and intentionality.

The serenity prayer provides a great mission statement to those unhappy in their current situation. We can seek to find out what is making us unhappy at work. We can then decide which things we have an ability to influence and which we do not. For those things we can influence, we should start doing so immediately. For those issues we cannot influence, we should decide if we can be at peace with things as they are. If we cannot, we may want to change our environment.

Change is at the core of human essence. It's natural. I once participated in a Q&A interchange on personal change with Marshall Goldsmith. Someone asked Goldsmith if people ever really change. He replied in the affirmative but acknowledged changing *perception* is harder than changing *behavior*.

The failure to change, either behavior or perception, is traced as the root for much of our unhappiness.

People tend to get comfortable within their environment to the point that they fear that which is new, that which is unknown. We can challenge these people to remember their goals and dreams.

This doesn't mean they need to quit their job, although that certainly is an option. Changing one's environment can involve any of the following: changing positions within the company; changing locations within the company; changing career fields; going back to school; standing up to a negative workplace behavior; respectfully challenging a manager; and of course, resigning.

Some people succeed in changing their environment and thus become more engaged and work once again becomes something they value. Others succeed in changing their perspective to achieve a similar outcome. But many more don't try, or don't succeed, in either venture. Leaders incur an obligation to look after this latter set. They are the 70 percent surveys caution us about.

Acting here is the epitome of leadership. It's about taking care of people. And it's not always easy. If it was easy, employee happiness and engagement wouldn't be the problem that we know it to be. The truth is this is difficult stuff without any magic solution, other than leadership.

Pollsters have spent a great deal of effort to convince us there's a problem. Over the last decade, Gallup continues to report only about a third of our employees are engaged. Obviously, something isn't working here. I've read many of the studies and have worked with numerous companies working strategies to improve engagement. I'm not convinced these are solving the right problem.

The issue goes beyond engagement.

The real problem we're facing also includes commitment, passion, and creativity. We only get this larger picture by considering the whole system. It's impossible to fully understand the problem without considering the associated interdependencies. People's engagement, and therefore their perspective of their job, is directly dependent upon their perceptions of their workplace environment—one directly affects the other. To address the issue, we must drive to the root of the problem.

As stated earlier, I've taught formal problem-solving techniques for many years. The key to effective problem-solving is to ensure we're solving the *right* problem. As we dig deeper into the engagement issue to further define the problem, we'll eventually uncover that many of our workplaces have become environments absent of meaningful emotional connections. These interpersonal and meaningful relationships are not only critical to engagement but also to employee performance, productivity, and success. This is the real reason Gallup questions if we have a best friend at work.

EMPOWERMENT

Considering the strength of many over the strength of one, our journey to excellence requires intentional actions to effectively empower the people. And while leaders must agree to bestow this empowerment, the employees must be willing to accept it. Sometimes neither is our reality.

We previously discussed how victimhood can keep a company from excellence. The solution here is leadership. Effective leaders empower employees to become confident, responsible, and accountable for their behavior and actions. But empowerment is another word that is often used out of context.

We can all agree empowerment is a good thing. Fewer of us agree on what empowerment means and how to positively affect it in our companies. The dictionary tells us empowerment is the act of granting power, right, or authority to perform duties. Robert Quinn, co-developer of the Competing Values Framework, puts forth an explanation where he considers two virtually opposing views, one labeled *mechanistic* and the other *organic*.

The mechanistic view focuses on clarity, delegation, control, and accountability while the organic view focuses on risk, growth, trust, and teamwork. Quinn advises we prefer our bosses use an organic approach with us while we tend to take a mechanistic approach with our own subordinates. Like so many other things, our perspective here drives our perception.

Not only does perspective matter, so does interpretation of the *intent* to empower. Intangibles within the culture and work design result in different applications to achieve empowerment. Two areas of typical focus are job enlargement and job enrichment.

Job enlargement entails changing the job scope to include a larger breadth of work. An example would be expanding a bank teller's responsibilities from handling deposits and disbursements to include selling traveler's checks and certificates of deposit.

Job enrichment entails changing the scope to include a greater depth of work, especially when adding tasks previously conducted by management. Keeping with the same example, a bank teller that's empowered with job enrichment has the authority to help customers complete loan applications and then make a recommendation on loan approval.

We must seek to implement an environment that allows people to do their work and to think about how they do that work. We need to allow them the freedom to improve how that work gets done without seeking management approval. This is the essence of empowerment.

Making gains here often requires companies to document their operational definition of empowerment and for the leadership team to communicate their commitment to it. A certain amount of structure is also required. Empowerment involves the transfer of authority with a clear agreement and understanding about expectations, responsibilities, and boundaries.

Empowerment is a two-way street requiring interaction between leader and those being led. But understanding how to empower subordinates is a higher-order leadership skill that can be lacking in those otherwise competent. A leader's Emotional Intelligence (EQ) and ability to empathize with others is critical. And while we can improve our EQ with intentional effort over time, there's another approach that can return faster results.

Returning to perspective, many leaders aren't aware that employees don't feel empowered. This could be due to the difference in the mechanistic versus organic perspective or it could be due to a certain amount of fear towards openly sharing information with the leader.

I've worked with several senior leaders that wanted to do the right thing, but they gave off an aura of being unapproachable on certain subjects. This commonly leads to the emperor has no clothes dilemma. Such an environment holds back the company, the leader, and the people from excellence. The fix here can be a simple concept known as the "locker room."

Within the best sports teams, the locker room is an environment of trust and mutual respect. Bringing this concept into the business world, leaders can create a temporary safe environment where employees are free to speak up without retribution.

A locker room can be convened to discuss sensitive issues. In this environment, employees are empowered to speak their mind without fear of retaliation. Information discussed is often unavailable to the leader through other means. And any information provided is a gift. Implementing this simple practice can help a leader understand how to better empower those under their charge.

Empowerment is somewhat about letting go, but it doesn't equate to abandonment. Bestowing authority upon subordinates doesn't relinquish a leader of responsibilities inherent to their position. Empowered employees quickly develop a stronger commitment to the cause, but their competence will still need to develop on its own course. Each employee's competence and commitment in specific tasks need to be assessed and the appropriate leadership style applied.

Empowerment results in people having the freedom to act to accomplish what needs to get done and then to be accountable for the results. But companies don't empower their employees out of sheer goodwill. Doing so benefits the company as much as it does the employees, maybe even more so. A company with empowered employees reaches levels of productivity otherwise not achievable.

A company that empowers its employees is committed to continually improving the environment of those accomplishing the work. A company that does this is on its way to excellence. A company that does not is destined to mire in mediocrity.

ACCOUNTABILITY

My friend Eric is an amazing man. A Marine Corps fighter pilot and combat veteran, Eric has a huge heart. Many years ago, while finishing a successful turnaround effort, I had the opportunity to serve as Eric's leader. We ultimately lost contact as our lives pursued their intended courses.

Ten years later, Eric and I enrolled in the same graduate program. Our lives had taken different paths to arrive back at a common point.

Eric's path included remarrying several years following the loss of his wife. He and his new bride each brought an exceptional needs child to the marriage. As a testament to his servant nature, Eric co-founded a much-needed non-profit organization for parents of Down syndrome children. His organization is now one of the largest of its kind in Southern California, no doubt due to Eric's leadership.

One evening over dinner and a lively discussion on accountability, Eric related the following story about his special daughter, Hope. Sometimes Hope does things which her parents don't find desirable. This could be anything from spilling her cereal bowl to writing on the walls with a crayon. When questioned about her behavior, Hope looks her parents in the eyes and sheepishly admits, "I did it on purpose." The honesty of this admission is refreshing.

Admitting intentionality of purpose doesn't excuse bad behavior. But then again, doing so doesn't equal an excuse. It equates to accepting accountability for the action.

Eric and his wife now find themselves using this tactic, learned from their child, whenever one questions the other on a troublesome subject. Many arguments have been reduced to laughter and understanding based upon the wisdom gained from a child.

The origin of the word accountability stems from ancient Rome when senators choosing to vote would move into a circle to be counted. Accountability remains one of the fundamental aspects of leadership, but one that is frequently absent in its pure form. Far too many in leadership roles attempt to excuse behavior instead of accepting the accountability of their actions.

Some incorrectly believe they can delegate accountability. Responsibility for completing an action may be delegated, but the accountability for doing so may not. Accountability is pure and simple—all it requires is for one to own the commitment, nothing further.

Integrity, like accountability, is essential to and inextricable from leadership. The absence of integrity is an absence of leadership. Integrity is special in that it can't be taken away—it can only be given away. If we do give away our integrity, there are consequences.

We face choices and their consequences every day. We are often free to make our own choices, but we aren't free to ignore the consequences of our decisions. Accepting the consequences brings us back to accountability.

I make no apologies for my zealous position on accountability. Some may think my position too strong. I obviously don't and believe this to be a foot stomper, so I'll explain.

I've had the opportunity to lead organizations ranging from just a couple to several hundred people. Throughout these roles, I've found there's a constant associated with my success and those that I've led—the understanding and acceptance of accountability. I don't think it's possible to over-emphasize the importance of accountability and its correlation to success.

Accountability can be likened to one of the "rinsing your cottage cheese factors" Jim Collins identifies as fanatical behavior present in all great companies. Accepting accountability for our actions is strictly a human act. The acceptance of accountability forms the essence of our integrity. A refusal to accept the link between one's behavior and its consequences often ends up ruining an individual's life.

Collectively, denying accountability and consequences can destroy an organization.

Even in companies that understand and embrace accountability, confusion and ambiguity may be present surrounding who is *accountable* and who is *responsible* for specific activities. The same confusion can cloud who must be *consulted* vice merely *informed* of decisions for defined tasks. The more complex the organizational construct, the more ambiguity and confusion likely to be present. Ambiguity, duplication of effort, and lack of efficiency often reign in these complex environments.

Many years ago, research introduced me to a simple tool that helps remove much of this ambiguity through clarifying roles and responsibilities. The tool is called a RACI matrix and, as represented in Figure 8.1, is familiar to most leaders. While many may be familiar, I'm not convinced the matrix is always employed properly to return the intended benefit.

R – Responsible A – Accountable C – Consulted I – Informed	Business Leader	Sales Team	Project Manager	Business Analyst	Project Team	SMEs	Production	Quality Assurance	Logistics & Warranty
Analyze Requirements	C	R	A	R	C	C	I	C	I
Bid Project	C	A,R	C	C	R	I			
Develop Product	I		A		R	C	C	C	I
Build & Test Product	I		A		C	C	R	R	
Sell Product	I	A,R	C	I	I				I
Support Product	I		A		I	C		C	R

FIGURE 8.1

RACI matrix.

The true value of the matrix occurs during its construction. The tool identifies specific tasks matrixed to stakeholders. Building the matrix helps us think through and clarify these stakeholder roles. Each task is individually assessed, identifying who is responsible (R), who is accountable (A), who must be consulted (C), and who needs to be informed (I). The RACI matrix clarifies roles in the presence of ambiguity. Its use corrects misconceptions about *who* has ownership for *what*.

Most importantly, the matrix helps establish accountability. Since accountability can't be delegated, one and only one (A) is assigned for each task, but there can be multiple (R)s. An individual may be both accountable (A) and responsible (R) for completing a specific task. Plots for (C) and (I) are optional for any task, and there can be more than one individual assigned for each.

The RACI matrix is a simple tool. Its application should remain simple and straightforward. When I've seen the matrix struggle to add value, it's often because the approach is over-complicated. I've observed organizations add additional parameters to the R-A-C-I structure. While the intent may be good, such practice distracts from its simplicity. I've also seen organizations create matrices of such depth that printed versions took up an entire conference room wall. If the detail bypasses mental associations, then the intent has been lost. Simpler is always better.

Organizations are increasingly interested in attempting to measure and classify a *culture of quality*. Many believe this concept represents desired characteristics within "the way things get done around here" that serve the customer. I argue a better option for pursuing excellence is to seek a *culture of accountability*.

There's a direct link between accountability and results.

Before we can move forward in healthy relationships and fully participate with others, we must be accountable to ourselves. This is the only path to holding others accountable. And our teams, which are of ever-increasing importance, won't be successful if they don't understand and embrace accountability.

TEAMWORK AND INDIVIDUALISM

Teams are the basic unit of performance in most companies. This truth is becoming more so the case every year. Our schools have transitioned to teaching our future leaders, starting in grade school, with team-based learning. But I'm starting to wonder, is this always the best solution?

Responding to change needed to achieve excellence requires teams with the competencies to deal with known and unknown challenges. These teams are typically cross-functional with expertise across several functional areas. They should be experts at current problems and prepared to cope with other challenges yet to be revealed.

A diverse team is almost always better qualified for the challenges we now face in our businesses. A team not enriched with diversity is often unaware of its limitations and the narrowed lens which it views and attempts to solve problems. We don't always self-recognize when our teams don't meet these requirements.

Sometimes, it takes an outsider to point out the obvious.

Several years ago, I was part of a team providing classified technical support to the US government. This team was many things. Diverse was not one of them. After a particularly frustrating discourse over not meeting their requirements, they let us know their thoughts on our diversity.

The leader bluntly informed us of their growing lack of confidence in our ability to understand and meet their needs. His exact words included the analogy that our leadership team was "too pale, too stale, and too male."

Changes to our organizational construct soon followed.

But changing our diversity make-up wasn't the only change needed. Our team had fallen into the trap that silently inflicts many teams and almost always without their knowledge. We were organized as a team and performed all work exclusively within this team structure.

There's a tremendous amount of information available that discusses productivity and improved results available through effective teamwork. The flood of information here is almost a one-way street. No one seems to be advocating against teams. I even claimed one of the keys to realizing Operational Excellence is the effective use of teams. And I stand behind that assessment. But there's another side of the coin we must also consider.

The use of teams has been steadily increasing over the last century. This began with the Hawthorne studies examining the psychological aspects of human behavior in organizations. Their use then exploded to become an inherent requirement about 30 years ago, with the proof documented through several best-selling books.

As the use of team's increased, our organizational constructs changed to accommodate them. We even changed our office seating plans to facilitate team needs. But we're now beginning to understand these actions may not always return the best results. We may need to unlearn some ideas about teams.

Effective teamwork is an important element to achieving excellence. But no activity should be organized exclusively into teams. Everything doesn't require a team. Sometimes, improved performance is best achieved by an individual. The most effective constructs now recognize the importance of dedicated time and space for individual contributions away from the team.

Susan Cain's best-selling book *Quiet* provides valuable research into some things we may have been getting wrong. Cain's work is exceptional in exploring how introverts see the world and how our movement towards teams has been stifling contributions for more than a third of our employees.

For a long time, many of us believed teams provided the best solutions for key organizational tasks. Problem-solving was one of those tasks. Within my problem-solving training, I included theory and studies that show the power of solving problems in teams over individuals. But after reading Cain's work, I began to question my conclusion.

What I've come to realize, and confirmed through studies and works such as *Quiet*, is that teams may not always offer the only solution. The best solution is often a hybrid that combines teamwork with individual effort. And it's not only true for problem-solving but across our collaboration efforts. By allowing people to work collaboratively, but then also providing individual time for those needing solitude to flourish, we can return results far greater than with teams alone.

Multiple studies have recently examined this trend and substantiated errors in our former approach. They've explored how introverts have been held back and how they can achieve higher performance. Others have examined how the interactions between high and low performers can both increase when provided an environment alternating between individual work and teaming.

While I'm a believer in the value of teams, I'm also an introvert and value my time alone to process and think. And I've always been suspicious of group think affecting our results. Coupled with this, I've become more aware of the tendency for those that are more articulate or aggressive to dominate the decisions and actions by teams. Those that talk the loudest or the fastest aren't always the same people with the best ideas.

Moving closer to excellence requires that we consider everyone's thoughts and ideas, even the introverts.

9

Improving Our Processes

Processes are how we work. Yet we all don't interpret the term *process* with the same definition.

We get different explanations when reviewing authoritative writings on the subject, such as Davenport's *Process Innovation*, Harrington's *Business Process Improvement*, or Juran's self-titled *Juran on Planning for Quality*. The common theme among these sources is that a *process* is a set of related activities that establish how we work and which produce a resulting value to the customer.

The familiar concept of *input-process-output* relates how we transform resources into products. But this also identifies a hidden shortcoming. We sometimes focus on the internal workings of the system to the point of ignoring the external environment. When companies internally focus, they eventually lose touch with the external environment and the customer. This creates a problem. Customer needs and wants must be the central focus of process design and generation.

Let's now take a closer look at the direction we're providing around these processes.

OUR WRITTEN RULES FOR HOW WORK GETS DONE

Developing new ideas and thinking is one way an organization grows and adapts to move towards excellence. Changing process is another. To paraphrase Albert Einstein, we're not going to solve our current problems with the same thinking that created our problems. New ideas, new customers, new technology, and new ways of thinking require new processes and procedures that are agile and adaptive to the demands of an ever-changing business environment.

The importance of developing and maintaining efficient processes and documented procedures cannot be over-stated. They drive the efficacy of our companies. When intentionally designed, these processes and procedures directly impact far-reaching elements of the business, to include:

Improving morale and engagement	Aligning activities to strategic goals
Obtaining consistent and predictable results	Facilitating training and employee onboarding
Reducing costs and improving competitiveness	Predicting and responding to system changes
Reducing errors and nonconformance	Improving problem-solving discipline

Typically, policies define the rules, those things within our companies that must be done or not done. Procedures define *who* does *what*, and lower level documents, such as instructions, provide specific direction for *how* the work is done.

Documents that are higher level and tied to strategic goals also discuss *why*. These are our core processes, the set of related and interdependent key activities that must be performed in an exemplary manner to transform inputs to outputs that add value to the customer. Core processes are at the center of what drives organizational behavior.

We often talk of value streams in the continuous improvement world. The original value stream in any organization is the stream of value created from the customer's point of view. Everything that directly contributes to this is part of a core process. Everything else is not.

All companies have some form of documented instructions for how work is accomplished. The organization of these documents varies greatly.

One of the better ways to organize written rules is through a common process architecture. Such an architecture aligns efforts across different sites and business areas. An intentional architecture provides the framework for disciplined and planned growth. When designing an architecture and documents to govern our business, we would be well-served to remember the parable of Occam's Razor. The simplest solution is often the best solution.

I've written and reviewed hundreds of procedures to document organizational process. Some of those procedures were quite good. Others were not, especially early in my career. And there's a reason why.

We have a tendency when writing, especially with formal written procedures, to try and sound too smart. The result is lengthy, drawn-out documents that create ambiguity and confusion. The best procedures are those written in simple, plain language that take the most direct route to providing direction.

Poorly written procedures create ambiguity, impact efficiency, and affect employee morale. And in extreme cases, they can lead to malicious compliance and normalized deviance.

Several years ago, I read an obscure little book on writing that changed my perspective for how we communicate written direction to employees. Verlyn Klinkenborg's *Several Short Sentences About Writing* informs, "If you write ambiguous sentences, you create a state of uncontrolled implication." He was discussing writing in general. But within our procedural documents, the resulting unintended consequences *will* impact the business, one way or another.

Our written procedures provide formal direction. Their authority is typically inferred from the level of authority of the document owner. A policy statement from the company president is promulgated under the authority of the president, an HR procedure by the authority of the head of HR, and an engineering instruction by the leader of engineering.

These things are obvious. But let's pause to examine the definition of *authority*.

The dictionary indicates authority as the "power to influence or command thought, opinion, or behavior." Klinkenborg provides another perspective. He informs us that authority is derived from clarity of language and clarity of perception. Molding these definitions together helps us improve process execution through better written direction.

A certain degree of trust develops between a writer and a reader. When our documented procedures are clear, precise, and absent of ambiguity, the likelihood of building trust increases. When we write better procedures, we create a path that will improve the trust between those establishing the rules and those expected to follow them. It's a path that will help our companies move closer to excellence.

But we often make things much harder than they need to be. When doing so, we suffer from self-inflicted inefficiencies. These occur more often than many of us may realize.

Throughout my career, I've often found the ability to make value-added improvement simply by challenging the rules that we operate within. I've been able to do so in my leadership roles within the private sector, the government, and the military. Each of these sectors has its own form of bureaucracy that tends to stifle innovation, decision-making, and sometimes, just doing the right thing.

Organizations often design their rules in a manner that hold them back from success. This occurs when rules aren't crafted as guidelines but as absolutes. Too many of our rules dictate exactly how we should or should not complete a task. While some rules may be so critical that they need to be absolute, these are the exception. We have too many black and white areas and not enough gray.

Rather than writing absolute rules, we should create written rules to be adaptive. Managers can then interpret the guidelines and provide direction to clarify gray areas.

Complicating the situation, many of our rules simply aren't well written, focused, or in the frankest of terms, good. Poorly written procedures hold our employees back from delivering value and great performance to our customers.

But poor procedures affect more than just our customers. They're the root cause for much of the inefficiency within our companies.

Poorly designed procedures cause people to work harder instead of smarter. Procedures often continue to grow and become more and more cumbersome and bureaucratic. Those perceiving the rules as irrational may start working around the procedures and, then eventually, ignoring them completely. This creates an entirely different problem. And one that we must now discuss.

WHY GOOD PEOPLE DO BAD THINGS

An organization that fails to follow its own procedures eventually experiences significant problems. Permitted to continue, the manifestation degrades to the point that deviance from expected conduct becomes normal behavior. As discussed earlier, such a scenario is called *normalized deviance.* This is a different problem and one that can devastate a culture. It's an impact of such magnitude that those affected may never fully recover.

In addition to normalized deviance, poor procedures can create an environment of malicious compliance. When employees disagree with how they're directed to accomplish their work, they can inflict intentional harm by following direction to the letter, even when they know it will return negative results. Just like normalized deviance, this is more of a leadership problem than a problem with any specific documented procedure.

An abundance of poor procedures and ignoring procedures each create serious issues. Leadership is the solution for both. Processes and procedures are intertwined within the culture and the way things get done. They help form the structure of our systems. Poor procedures therefore result in poor structures. The impact to our efficiency and effectiveness is quite real.

Procedural inefficiencies are one of the largest contributors to the delta between the current and desired culture that will enable us to achieve excellence. Simply put, poor procedures keep employees from doing their jobs the way they know the jobs should be done. A collection of poor procedures strips employees of their empowerment.

Some companies claim to have empowered employees that serve the customer. But they have rules in place that work against this intent. The result prevents employees from enacting the vision and therefore, impedes the company's path to excellence.

My management focus has been in the quality field for most of my career. Within these roles, I've had the inherent responsibility to ensure compliance. From a quality management standpoint, compliance refers to meeting legal requirements, such as statutory or regulatory laws. Conformance is less formal and applies to conforming to the elements of a specification or standard, such as ISO 9001.

While compliance and conformance are both necessary, we're seeking an environment of committed employees. A committed workforce defaults to compliant behavior. But there are exceptions. And often, employees may not even realize they're acting outside of the rules.

Our employees want to do the right things. We need to author the direction for them to accomplish their work that allows them to do so and without being overly prescriptive. When we over-prescribe direction for how to accomplish work, we risk micro-managing those who seek to deliver results that draw on their own creativity and ingenuity.

And just like we don't want to create overly prescriptive procedures, we need to be diligent against creating too many procedures. *Administrivia* describes the accumulation of many cumbersome, complicated, and non-value-added rules. These rules grow out of the structures of our systems. While structure is important, too much structure is seldom a good thing.

Sometimes, these structures increase to the point that they can become shackles.

Without an intentional intervention, the number of documented procedures will never decrease but assuredly continue to increase. The accumulation of such process more often than not ends up departing from their original intended purpose. In these environs, leaders must assess the message and ensure the focus of process remains on providing value to the customer. Unfortunately, as organizations mature, processes often pivot to serve internal functions more than the customer.

Among the best procedures an organization can enact is one that permits waiving or deviating from a process. This is especially so in highly structured organizations, such as manufacturing, finance, and aviation. It's not a "get out of jail free card," but it does provide a process to employ logic and reason when written direction doesn't consider common sense or the proper action to take in a given situation.

Applied properly, a simple waiver system can go a long way towards simplifying other procedures and ensuring compliance. And it provides the conduit for specificity, agility, and accountability on our path to excellence.

PROBLEM-SOLVING

As the world becomes increasingly more complex, companies are facing problems never previously envisioned. Our problems range from a simple defect in a product to dealing with a global pandemic and a locked-down workforce. The larger the problem, the more important our ability to solve it. And to be competitive, we must do so faster and with more effectiveness.

All companies have problems. Our effectiveness in recognizing and dealing with these problems and then learning from them serves as our *true* sustainable competitive advantage. Problem-solving at its essence is learning. Effective problem-solving starts with transparency. Human nature leads us away from admitting we have problems. But if there are no problems, there's no opportunity for improvement.

In our global marketspaces of constant change, we're increasingly seeking how to do more with less. No one does more with less. We do less with less. The only way we can do more is if we weren't providing a full effort before and then decided to do so now.

But we're constantly challenged to do more within a modern world that continues to transform from an industrial to a knowledge base. A company that blinks may miss the entire life cycle of a given technology. These *things* are happening faster and with more frequency. And they aren't all positive.

Economic and market instabilities are increasing realities that are here to stay. They create obstacles that oppose our movement to excellence. To meet the challenges, risks, and opportunities these situations create, companies must be intentional about improving their ability to solve problems. The best companies will be ones creating a culture that prioritizes and reinforces problem-solving as a habit.

This isn't a talent that some people have and others do not—effective problem-solving is a habit we all can develop. But far too often, we focus on correcting symptoms instead of identifying the root causes and correcting them at the source. This latter approach always requires a larger initial investment of time, but the benefit from having to solve the problem only once makes the return worth the effort.

Emplacing a structured problem-solving process is simple. And it's only four steps, as indicated in Figure 9.1.

The initial step seeks to understand the current situation and clearly define the problem to be fixed. This is the most important step. As we define the problem, it's vitally important that we consider the system under analysis. The system we define around the problem will influence the ultimate cause we identify. Here, it's vital that we acknowledge our

 Define Problem to be Solved

 Identify the Root Cause of the Problem

 Develop & Implement Corrective Actions

 Verify Effectiveness of the Solution

FIGURE 9.1

Problem-solving process.

biases and assumptions about the problem. These will frame our understanding of the problem and our ultimate identified cause.

Time spent defining the problem is critical, even if done at the expense of time remaining to solve the problem. Defining the problem begins with developing a problem statement. This simple statement relates the specific undesired condition and its resulting impact. If we consider sickness as an example, the problem statement may be "Fever causing chills and elevated body temperature."

The second step is to find the root cause of the undesired condition. Admittedly, root cause analysis is both an art and a science and something that's hard to do. But competence in this skill is a differentiator for companies that seek to achieve excellence.

Root cause analysis seeks to trace the problem back to the first event in the chain leading to the undesired condition. For our sickness example, we conduct analysis to explore beyond the symptoms to find the root of the problem, identified as a bacterial infection.

The third step in the problem-solving process is to develop and implement corrective actions to prevent the undesired condition from recurring. Enacting corrective actions for the root cause keeps the entire sequence from repeating. If we err when identifying the root cause, actions taken here become merely corrections to symptoms. For our example, taking aspirin is a correction that addresses the symptoms. Taking antibiotics to address the infection is the corrective action.

The last step of the process is to verify effectiveness of the developed solution set. This requires the problem solver revisit the problem after a set period and verify the undesired condition hasn't reappeared. We validate the corrective actions are now the new way of doing things. Within our simple example, this is a follow-up visit to the doctor to confirm the infection has been eliminated.

Whereas defining the problem is the most critical step, finding the root cause is clearly the most difficult step. I've taught root cause analysis techniques for many years across the military, government, and private sector and as a lecturer at professional conferences. The students have come from all functional disciplines. One observation has remained consistent— most of us aren't very good at root cause analysis.

There's an impact here. Absence of a trained bench in effective problem-solving inhibits organizational learning and the ability to deal with the unknown presented by the future.

I found an absence of the skill in areas where it should have been a core competency, such as engineering and production environments. This confused me, so I set out to find the root cause of ineffective root cause analysis.

I'm not kidding, I did this. What I found from this investigation, I've since confirmed to be repeated across many organizations and disciplines. My investigation revealed two primary findings.

My first finding was those expected to explore the cause of failures often default to mental heuristics to bucket problems into instead of conducting formal analysis. Over time, these mental shortcuts, initially driven by perceived time constraints, become the norm and replace the process of formal cause analysis. This phenomenon has proved itself in most every organization that I've served.

To address this, we must unlearn the use of our mental shortcuts. Finding root cause is one of those areas that requires we slow down to go fast.

The second finding goes back to the importance of having proper problem definition. Our consideration of the system and our inherent biases and assumptions affect our ability to solve the right problem. People don't naturally apply systems thinking, but it's paramount to problem-solving.

I used the example of a squirrel and his surrounding environment when I introduced systems thinking. I use this same example in my problem-solving training. Imagine the squirrel has died and your job is to identify the cause. The system we define will directly affect the cause we identify. If our system is just the squirrel, our conclusions will focus on his internal systems which failed and led to death. If our system considers the squirrel and the forest he lives in, our findings would be very different.

Similarly, the preconceptions we have about organizational life, to include our own personal biases and assumptions, drive the effectiveness of our problem-solving, starting with how we define the problem. Back in our culture discussion, I emphasized the importance of beliefs. And these beliefs are formed by our underlying assumptions. We must not discount the impact of these assumptions on our ability to define the problem we want to solve.

Common tools and applications are available to help us identify the root cause. These are helpful. But they're useless without the right thought process behind them. These tools are only frameworks to assist in the process. Much more important are the thought processes we use to drive understanding of the problem, to include those identified below:

To be curious, inquisitive, and creative	To be aware of biases and assumptions
To seek answers to penetrating questions	To use both synthesis and analysis
To be logical and analytical	To think beyond either/or to both/and thinking
To apply convergent and divergent thinking	To think and see things in terms of the system

Another common problem I find with many approaches is the tendency to blame people. Fancy words and adjectives are often placed around the identified cause, but if we remove these, it reveals we are blaming *someone* for doing it wrong. Such conclusions are almost always incomplete.

Why did the operator do it wrong? If determined to be intentional, that is an entirely different problem to be addressed through other means, to include Human Resources. Such cases are the rare exception.

But I've often found "human error" as the leading cause identified by organizations immature in their problem-solving. Effective problem-solving isn't about blaming people. It's about determining what's broken within the system and implementing process improvements to keep the problem from repeating.

Becoming better at problem-solving is now more important than ever. Doing so not only helps separate us from our competitors, it can be the difference in a company surviving in this new world. This alone is reason enough to pursue a larger and more effective bench of problem solvers.

We're seeking to make problem-solving a habit, for this desire to become contagious across the company to help us on our path to excellence.

10

Realizing Our Products

The core of what our companies do is provide products and services that serve our customers. This is the output of everything discussed to this point.

WHY DOMINATES WHAT

It's been more than a decade since Simon Sinek first turned our thinking upside down with his acute insight into how we inspire people. He changed our perspective for how we view our customers and how they view us, the companies that provide their products and services. Sinek's language has quickly become standard corporate speak. The ideas from his books and talks are well known and now help drive new thoughts into how we run our companies.

I'll assume Sinek's influence is near complete for those interested in such things, and that *why* a company does what it does is recognized as more important than *what* it does. Some may not be onboard with that conclusion. But to be fair, we've already acknowledged that every company won't be able to achieve excellence.

Sinek's most famous ideas focus on our beliefs for a company's *why* and how that influences our behavior as potential customers. But our understanding of *why* also influences our behavior as employees within our companies through our underlying assumptions.

In the earlier discussion of process, I stated core processes are those things the company must complete in an exemplary manner to deliver value to the customer. The documented procedures for core processes include clarifying *why* to help employees understand their importance to the business.

But this importance to understand *why* transcends to even more fundamental levels. Individual employees completing routine tasks in support of the company's mission must understand *why* they do what they do. Understanding *why* improves the quality and efficiency of their work product.

I once led operations at a manufacturing plant that built engines for military vehicles. During final assembly, the oil coolers were sometimes installed "inside-out." The parts were near symmetrical and nothing in the process precluded mis-installation. The error wasn't uncommon and when occurring, resulted in rework and production delays.

At the time, we had an aggressive continuous improvement leader that wanted to poka-yoke the operation. His ideas would have worked. They also would have required significant resources to implement. But there was an easier solution. And a better solution.

The oil coolers were near symmetrical, but not quite. One face of the coolers, meant to be installed towards the engine, had thin and fragile heat transfer fins. The other face, intended to face outward, had much thicker fins designed to withstand the harsh environment experienced by military vehicles.

Rather than error-proof the installation process, we decided a better solution was to provide the operators system-level training on the engine and its final application. Through learning gleaned from this training, the operators now understood why this part was to be installed a certain way.

We didn't need to document pages of additional procedures or design any new tooling to get them to improve their performance. We explained why. And we never had an oil cooler mis-installed again.

DESIGN THINKING

Steve Jobs told us to design how it works, not how it looks. As we design our products to add value for the customer, there's a non-traditional methodology that goes beyond just hoping that we improve the customer experience.

Design thinking originated as an approach to designing products and services through focusing on customer perception, needs, and wants during the concept development phase. It's a simple three-step process: *discover, define,* and *develop.* The methodology emphasizes empathy with the user. It departs from other methodologies by intentionally delaying problem definition until better understanding the customer perspective.

Discover entails observing the customer and empathizing with them to understand their situation. Divergent thinking helps us develop different choices to consider alternative solutions as confirmed through observation. We transition to convergent thinking to *define* the problem once understood from the user point of view. And then we transition back to divergent thinking to *develop* and ideate potential solutions. We then prototype, test, and repeat until convergent thinking helps us deliver an acceptable solution.

Although often identified by its three-step process, design thinking may be better explained as a system of spaces, consisting of the "problem space" and the "solution space" as indicated in Figure 10.1.

Some have likened design thinking as an attempt to package creativity within a process format. While this provides insight to the framework, it also provides a hint of its potential limitations.

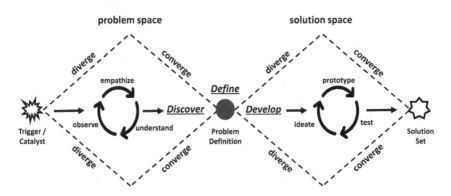

FIGURE 10.1

Design thinking.

Attempts to package creativity as a linear process can hope to be moderately successful, at best. As a formal methodology, standalone success rates admittedly aren't very robust. The framework adds the most value when its approach is integrated to support other continuous improvement methodologies.

I attended an event on design thinking about ten years ago featuring Jane Chen, founder and CEO of Embrace India. Chen spoke on her company's ability to bring desperately needed incubator blankets to the Third World. Faced with high infant mortality rates and a severe shortage of incubators, Chen's team solved the problem through assessing the situation from the customer's perspective.

The root of the problem was mothers were distrustful of others. The inevitable result was low birth weight babies in rural areas weren't getting to the hospital in time for medical attention.

Chen's solution provided mothers an insulated pouch they could heat by adding hot water to a removable pad. Even the most distrustful mother didn't fear this simple process. Her team solved the problem through empathizing with the customer's needs to develop a creative solution. They did so for one percent of the cost of a normal incubator. With these lower costs, Chen's team was able to provide 100 times the number of solutions to their desperate customers.

Some may question what a discussion on design thinking has to do with Operational Excellence. Let me clarify. Design thinking has *everything* to do with Operational Excellence. Design thinking helps us understand customer needs. The threat of subconsciously moving away from customer needs is real. Incorporating this kind of thinking provides a powerful stimulant to keep our focus on the customer.

A specialized area of Six Sigma, referred to as Design for Six Sigma (DFSS), focuses on improving product design. This process employs analysis and statistics coupled with the familiar DMAIC (Define, Measure, Analyze, Improve, and Control) model. Some are now combining design thinking and DFSS to improve the design process through a blend of art and science. In fact, many traditional Lean Six Sigma certification programs now include modules on design thinking.

When we decide to pursue excellence, new ideas and thoughts will be required. Design thinking coupled with other improvement systems will help us here. We need to move beyond our traditional tools, pre-defined thoughts, assumptions, and checklists for solving our customer's problems. We need to apply new thinking and new tools to help us develop new solutions.

A year after Chen's presentation, I was in Istanbul sharing a bottle of wine with a well-known professor, Dr. Jaime Gomez. We stumbled onto a discussion of design thinking. Dr. Gomez had been working to get several universities to incorporate these ideas into their MBA programs but without success. As we enjoyed the wine, his frustration with academia's short-sightedness was more than apparent.

Several years later, Dr. Gomez was promoted to Dean of the School of Business at the University of San Diego. I wasn't surprised to see the University soon begin to embrace this design thinking idea.

Design thinking is conceptual and uses atypical methodologies. The method itself isn't what's important. What is important is the need to teach our leaders and thinkers new thought processes that draw on non-standard concepts such as empathy, compassion, and systems thinking to solve the future challenges that will be present in our pursuit of excellence.

INNOVATION

Some companies approach innovation the way some leaders approach humility. Simply stating we are innovative, or even aligning it to an espoused value, does nothing to infuse innovation as part of our culture, of "the way things get done around here." To have a culture of innovation is to have employees perceive that the organization supports innovation and responds positively to ideas-based change derived from innovative thought.

Innovation can drive change, such as realized through design thinking. Change can also drive innovation, such as realized by strategic plans with their breakthrough objectives and new ways of thinking.

But innovation is a broad word that will always mean different things to different people. It can range anywhere from small improvements achieved through kaizen, up through transformational change to our products, services, and even our business models.

Traditional Lean thinkers tend to believe that kaizen are the everyday improvement activities while innovation involves larger and more strategic initiatives. I would agree with that. But they also tend to believe that kaizen is people-oriented while innovation is money- or technology-oriented. I would disagree with that.

If innovation only required money, then the wealthiest companies would be the most innovative. That is hardly the case. And while technology is important to innovation, people develop that technology. Innovation is very much people focused.

Succeeding at innovation requires more than just the requisite technical and analytic skills. The culture must openly embrace innovation, else it will be short-lived. We need to think of innovation as an inherent political activity, as it can threaten the status quo. It may even be perceived as a threat. It's critical to be aware of these undertones when implementing ideas-driven change as we move towards excellence.

The role of the leader is to provide a safe environment for innovation to thrive.

Maslow's hierarchy of needs helps us understand the importance of this safe environment. Change presents the unknown. Pursuing excellence results in transformational change and a great deal of unknown. Bold effort will be required to create what doesn't exist. If those affected have unsatisfied physiological and safety concerns, there's little hope of them moving forward. We must first satisfy these basic needs.

We can then address their belonging and esteem needs for innovation to become a path for the new way things get done around here. And we do this through creating a safe environment.

A safe environment helps encourage new ideas and new ways of thinking. It allows people to experiment and think differently without retribution. A safe environment includes frequent explaining and communication by leadership throughout the change process. And a safe environment has barriers emplaced to protect people from harm, especially in those areas perceived to be threatening.

Think about a caring parent teaching their child to ride a bike.

We could plot most any child's commitment and competency for the task. My bet is the plot would mirror the standard change curve. We can take this example a little deeper and discover the parent's leadership style would follow the path predicted by situational leadership. Their leadership would likely start out as directive, explaining the bike and what to do and not do, and then progress through coaching, supporting, and finally to delegating once the child masters the task.

Now think about the parent's behavior along the way. Mistakes are not followed by punishment. But each positive achievement is surely met with enthusiastic praise and celebration. The act of rewarding without punishing increases competence and commitment from the new rider. It also helps reduce the time needed to master the skill.

This process of creating a safe environment and then realizing greater rewards faster is a wonderful thing. In business, it's also a rare thing, except in those companies that have achieved excellence.

Innovation is important. But we can't teach people to be innovative. Well, let me correct that. We can train them on concepts such as innovation sprints, but real innovation comes from within.

No one knows how our business models will change in our new world. But I believe it's safe to predict innovation will become even more important. While we can't predict the future and plan for things that are yet to come, we can ensure that we're creating the safe environment where innovation can thrive.

QUALITY ASSURED

I've been an advocate of improved quality since the late 80s. That's when I landed my first quality role, an internship analyzing failures in ferrite transistors at a manufacturing plant. The job was quality control—screening out good product from bad. But I was more interested in what made them good or bad and what could be affected within the process to make more of them good.

I've since held quality roles of manager, director, and vice president across several large companies. Within the military, I held quality roles ranging from QA Officer for a detachment up to QA Officer for the Atlantic Fleet Naval Air Forces. One thing remained consistent in each of these roles—my curiosity for why things are the way they are and how we can make them better.

Gone are the days where Quality's role was limited to inspection of product to ensure conformance. Quality must now be engaged throughout the value stream to assure quality at the source. In this environment, the leadership role of Quality can be understated. The most forward-looking companies recognize the importance of uncompromised quality and leverage it as a competitive advantage and discriminator. Everyone in a formal Quality role is in a leadership position. And everyone in a formal leadership role is a representative of Quality.

Enhancing the role of Quality beyond inspection isn't a new idea. Thirty-five years ago, Masaaki Imai identified in his famous book *KAIZEN* that people in a quality role are defined by being a facilitator, informer, trainer, and trust-builder.

In today's marketspaces, quality can be a valued discriminator and catalyst for optimizing costs and efficiency. Quality professionals pursuing excellence must obtain training and certifications to meet these increasing demands. Below are several common characteristics we should be seeking in our quality professionals:

- a professional with business acumen and understanding of the larger business model
- a driven expert who leads process improvement initiatives with an enterprise focus
- a champion that understands the importance of teams *and* individual effort
- a systems thinker with expertise in risk thinking and knowledge management tools

- a breakthrough thinker who understands the connection to the broader marketspace
- a problem solver that believes in measuring and improving everything

This book began by discussing the professional quality community's movement towards this concept of excellence. While this movement is real, it doesn't discount the continuing need for quality as a function. Quality is but one necessary function on the journey to excellence. Quality professionals may initially champion this movement to excellence, but senior leadership must become the leading advocate.

For a long time, I've maintained the professional mantra of *improve quality, reduce costs*. Improving quality is one of the <u>best</u> ways we can improve sustained profits on our journey to excellence. This requires we engage and improve quality across the entire value stream. Figure 10.2 identifies the familiar cost impacts of delaying quality, either intentionally or unintentionally.

A common metric across many companies attempts to measure the cost of quality and its impact to operations. While often referred to as the cost of quality (CoQ), many companies are only measuring a subset of the CoQ.

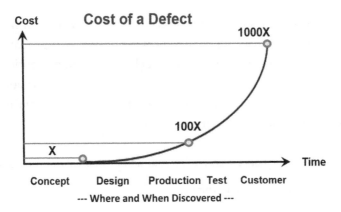

FIGURE 10.2

Impact of delaying quality.

What they're often measuring is only the cost of poor quality (CoPQ), which are the costs associated with nonconformance from *internal* and *external failures*. These costs include the typical criteria of rework, repair, defects, warranty repairs, customer returns, and test failures.

On its own, the CoPQ is an incomplete metric. It won't deliver the system solution necessary to achieve excellence. Remember, the purpose of a metric is to modify behavior. By limiting our aperture to only the cost of nonconformance, we're missing the opportunity to assess and optimize those behavior levers that influence these costs, reported as the cost of conformance.

Companies focusing on the CoPQ without assessing the whole CoQ are like a football team fielding both an offense and defense but limiting their attention for recruiting, training, practice, and gameday preparation to <u>just</u> the defense. Such a team may be great at defending, but its ability to take the initiative and influence the game through offensive action would be limited to luck.

And it would surely be an average team, at best.

Expanding our aperture to the system, we're interested in much more than just the cost of nonconformance, or CoPQ. We're equally interested in the cost of conformance, which includes *appraisal* and *prevention* activities, such as internal audits, testing, and continuous improvement efforts.

By monitoring and measuring the cost of conformance *and* the cost of nonconformance, we can adjust the levers to produce favorable results. We can increase the cost of conformance, such as through prevention activities, to return a favorable reduction in the cost of nonconformance, such as internal failures. This approach requires that we view the entire system and each of the associated interdependencies.

Cost of Nonconformance = cost of internal failures + cost of external failures

CoPQ = total cost of nonconformance

Cost of Conformance = cost of appraisal activities + cost of prevention activities

CoQ = total cost of nonconformance + total cost of conformance

Of all the metrics we can develop to measure improvement on our journey to excellence, the CoQ is possibly the most influential. Done correctly, this metric and the new behavior it generates can change the game.

CoQ isn't a metric limited to the manufacturing sector. It applies to almost every industry, especially those maintaining certification to an industry standard. ISO identifies 39 discrete industry sectors for companies seeking certification to their quality management system standard. These range from the *Agriculture, Fishing, and Forestry* sector to the *Health and Social Work* sector. Each of these sectors has opportunities to measure and improve their costs associated with internal and external failures, appraisal, and prevention activities.

In 1987, Public Law 100–107 created the *Malcolm Baldrige National Quality Award*. Legislators recognized "that poor quality costs companies as much as 20 percent of sales and revenues." But again, this measure is the CoPQ. Expanding this to the CoQ, the numbers represent up to 40 percent of a company's revenue.

Considering this tremendous cost impact and our ability to affect it with reductions, one must wonder why the CoQ isn't more pronounced across industry. It should be *the* pinnacle cost metric reported up to the highest levels of the company, to include the board of directors.

But there's a reason it's not. And the cause has already been discussed.

The reason ties back to our discussion of management skills across the different levels in our hierarchies. Within the traditional structures of most mid-size and large companies, top management tends to limit their focus to financial efficiency, with virtually no concern for process efficiency. This is most odd, considering that the latter drives the former.

Senior executives often shy away from abandoning their conceptual skills world to one that requires more technical focus. They can struggle to understand the physical nature of process and the costs that govern their business. It is almost an intentional withdrawal from understanding, as if not having further insight will isolate them from needing to make the ensuing hard, and data-driven, decisions. While I wish this behavior was the exception, I fear that it's not.

While most metrics don't result in creating emotional responses, effective ones tied to the CoQ often do. Affecting change here requires transparency, something many senior leaders avoid as it exposes what's happening behind the curtain. Even though cost performance can dramatically improve, taking action to do so presents risk and loss of referent power. It is therefore avoided.

I have often introduced senior leadership to the ideas of a CoQ metric. Convincing some of them to make these changes has been one of the more challenging undertakings of my career. In every instance where I was successful, transparency by leadership was a valued trait. And this transparency was absent each time I was unsuccessful.

Managing these costs is now more important than ever. Companies that make the connection and implement a true CoQ metric are on their way to excellence. The many that don't will continue to make up our normal curve distribution for companies that maintain average performance.

Part IV

Things the Customer Sees

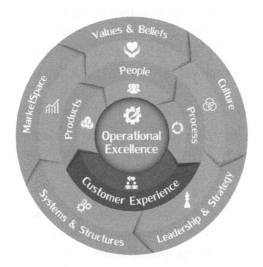

The best stories of great customer service are well known. There are legendary tales from companies like Zappos, Ritz Carlton, and Nordstrom that most of us have heard recounted many times. And there now are many new stories, soon to be legendary, telling of company heroics serving their customer during the coronavirus pandemic. But while this book, and this Part, does focus on that kind of relationship, my introduction here is going to pivot.

We can optimize the customer experience through four specific actions: doing the thing; being responsible; taking the initiative; and enabling an environment for others to thrive.

These aren't the typical actions we think of when we envision how to improve customer satisfaction. But these are the very things, if executed with precision and with passion, that will delight our customers and enhance their overall experience.

Doing the thing simply means completing our tasks. Doing them well. And consistently doing them to the best of our ability.

Being responsible results in ensuring what needs to get done, is done, and again, is done to the best of our ability. Our values and beliefs guide our actions here, not the conditions in which we find ourselves. There is no room for victimhood when discussing excellent customer service.

Taking the initiative results in action in the absence of direction. We seek to empower a team that understands and pursues the vision. We don't want a team that waits around to be told to do the thing. We want one that does so on their own, guided by their judgment, intuition, and situational awareness.

Finally, enabling an environment for others to thrive is one of the fundamental outputs from realizing Operational Excellence. Remember, we're seeking to continuously improve the environment for those accomplishing the work.

These four concepts above are derived from a short but famous article written more than 120 years ago, *A Message to Garcia*. I doubt we'll find these same ideas in any other leadership book discussing customer experience. But that doesn't change their relevance to the discussion.

11

Optimizing the Customer Experience

Optimizing the customer experience, defined as the product of interaction between an organization and a customer over the duration of their relationship, is the product of an operationally excellent company.

This interaction moves beyond just assessing satisfaction. Optimizing the customer experience means we also consider the customer's interest, awareness, cultivation, advocacy, purchase, and use of our products and services.

Within this definition, we need to sometimes consider a *customer* as not only those who buy our goods and services but also our internal customers and stakeholders, to include our employees and other interested parties.

Many of the most forward-leaning companies are now even seeking to delight their customers. *Why* not only dominates *what* we do, but in today's marketspace, customers have choices to the point that *what* we sell is no longer the discriminator. How well we sell it now often provides a more valuable discriminator. The company that delivers the best customer experience wins while it realizes excellence.

THE PURPOSE OF BUSINESS

If I posed the question, "What's the primary purpose of business?," many may answer to make money or to create shareholder value. I would disagree with both answers. Neither response provides enough justification for a business to remain in existence.

Over the last 20-plus years, America's most influential group of corporate leaders, the *Business Roundtable*, maintained a mission statement that declared "the paramount duty of management and of boards of directors is to the corporation's stockholders." By the middle of 2019, this group finally re-thought this approach with a statement of purpose that now begins with a commitment to "delivering value to our customers."

The purpose of a business is to serve the customer needs by providing goods and services needed by the customer. By-products of this purpose include making money and creating shareholder value. The more effective the business is at achieving its purpose, the more substantial these by-products become.

A company that thinks its purpose is to make money eventually begins to believe that its bottom line is more important than the customer. This can lead to temporary gains. But the longer-term outcome has little in common with excellence. Customers are the reason any business exists.

Taken to a more elementary level, the purpose of a business, even the purpose of individual employees within the business, is simply to add value. A business that doesn't add value to its customers is destined to fail. It follows that organizational effectiveness then is nothing more than a measure of this value.

Recall the story from the Introduction about the president who hired me to stimulate change. About a year into my role, he asked me to address the company at an all-hands meeting. He wanted me to discuss progress towards achieving our strategic goals. The plan was for the president to provide opening comments on financial performance, and then I would review our goals.

We were having a good year financially, although as previously mentioned, we were doing so by leveraging our future. The president finished his talk and handed me the microphone. Unfortunately, I erred and was mentally rehearsing my words. I hadn't paid attention to anything he said.

My opening statement questioned the employees on the purpose of our business. The rhetorical question was met with the expected silence, so I answered it myself. I emphasized the purpose of our business was not to make money, but to deliver value to our customers. I then walked through our Strategic Goal Deployment (SGD) performance and the value we provided to each of our key customers.

What I didn't realize was my opening words directly contradicted the president's closing remarks. As I learned later, he left the stage emphasizing our healthy profits and increased shareholder value. That explains the strange looks I received as I began my talk.

The president was a good man and a fine leader who I deeply respected. I learned a lot from him. But he was groomed under an old-school business philosophy that believed shareholders were more important than customers.

Within six months of that all-hands meeting, our largest customer fired us. This was the same customer we were struggling with on negotiations. Before we could fully affect our transition to excellence, the customer lost patience with our inability to meet their needs. It was a devastating lesson measured in hundreds of millions of dollars.

CUSTOMER ASSURANCE

Businesses that get it, that are high performing, integrate the customer throughout the value chain. They do this from the beginning. They start with a planning process that focuses on customer expectations.

Companies produce products from processes designed to customer needs. Processes that don't add value to the customer are waste. Everyone within the organization should understand their accountability to the customer and the notion that without the customer, there's no need for their business.

Most businesses start on a path focusing on the customer. Keeping on that path is a different story. Doing so can become difficult, especially as companies mature and their focus inevitably shifts inward.

This shift is a truth of business psychology. Many businesses attempt to measure customer satisfaction as a countermeasure to try and remain on the correct path. Common systems attempt to assess customer satisfaction through surveys, retention rates, net promoter scores (NPS), and other mathematical scoring systems.

The products resulting from such measurements are often of limited value. The reason is a common error in problem-solving. In this case, we're trying to determine the customer's satisfaction level. But we risk trying to solve the wrong problem because of a poor measurement approach. When we measure the wrong thing, we may try to modify the wrong behavior.

These approaches often lack an accurate assessment of the customer's initial satisfaction that we use to compare later measurements. Scientific research in this area is robust thanks to cognitive dissonance theory. A by-product of this theory, applicable to measuring customer satisfaction, is the expectancy disconfirmation theory (EDT).

Using EDT, we can represent the typical mechanics behind most measurement attempts. Keeping this simple, we'll assign independent variables to the customer's initial expectations (E) and their resulting perception of performance (P). The difference between these is the disconfirmation (D). Mathematically, $P - E = D$. Results producing a positive score for disconfirmation (D) indicate relative satisfaction. Negative scores indicate the relative dissatisfaction.

The problem with such an approach is not having a system in place to accurately assess initial expectations (E). Our assessments often have false assumptions. The math may indicate a positive satisfaction; reality often indicates otherwise. The ground truth is that we often fail to understand our customers.

Mathematics aside, fixing this requires new ways of looking at the problem. Let's consider some options that provide a different lens to view the problem.

Rather than focus on mathematical computations, we should instead consider what we've learned from assessing our own organizations. We previously discussed how we shouldn't ignore the impact of emotional thought in the workplace. Similarly, we err if we don't consider this variable in the customer's satisfaction with our products and services. Any attempt to measure customer satisfaction must include an assessment of their emotional connection to our products and services.

I developed a process to improve our understanding of delivered value and the customer's emotional connection with the product. The value measured is the perception by the customer, *within* their own environment. I refer to this as a VALUE assessment—an acronym for **V**alidation **A**ssessment **L**earned in a **U**ser **E**nvironment. The process conducts objective assessments *where* the customer uses the product. Lab equipment is fine for confirming product performance in a lab environment. But if we want to understand what the customer thinks of our products, we must observe them using the products.

The aerospace industry has a career field known as *mission assurance.* The mission assurance discipline is responsible for overall success and safety of products.

A key tenant of mission assurance is its independent nature that oversees task completion without undue influence and pressures. These pressures often originate from the functional elements and their inward focus. Those in mission assurance positions think differently. They usually have close customer intimacy, are empathetic to the customer's needs and wants, and represent the voice of the customer back to the organization.

Within our context of pursuing excellence, I propose these previous ideas combine into a new concept, referred to as *Customer Assurance*, to reconnect with our customer base. Implemented across an organization, Customer Assurance can become a galvanizing force to keep our focus on the customer.

Customer Assurance can move us beyond a simple tally of satisfaction to a focus that empathizes with the customer. It will seek to understand customer needs and wants and then take a leadership position to satisfy those needs and wants. Doing so will become a value discriminator the customer will notice. And it will discriminate excellent companies from those that choose to remain average.

INTERNAL versus EXTERNAL FOCUS

The philosopher Carl Jung's famous insight about looking inside to awaken applies to people, not our companies. Companies often fall prey to allowing their focus to eventually shift more and more inward.

An organization that focuses inward doesn't awaken—it is quickly obviated by the competition.

Many years ago, I was working with the federal government providing oversight on a defense contractor. The company had a great product. The customer's demand for the product was almost insatiable. The government was the only customer and the company had the market captured.

As often happens, price began to increase as concern for the customer began to decrease. The company started resisting customer-requested changes. They instead took the proverbial "build it and they will come" approach. What they really did was missed the opportunity to serve their customer.

Competition eventually increased.

The company is no longer the dominant force in the market. They chose to challenge their customer as to not knowing best. Their failure to focus on the customer proved to be an expensive lesson.

This company had some brilliant people. They made many changes to their product along the way. The problem was, management maintained a "cost-plus view of price" and few of these changes focused on reducing costs to reduce price and improve customer value.

Companies that don't focus on the customer often implement change for the wrong reasons. This is wasted effort and moves them further from satisfying their customer's needs and wants. We must always consider the customer when we design changes. We should be able to link any change to improvements realized by the customer, from cost reductions to product improvements. If we cannot, then it is likely change implemented for the wrong reason.

The ISO standard writers made a much-needed change with the latest revision of ISO 9001. They recognized a pattern of companies not focusing outward and failing to understand the context of their organizations in their marketspaces. ISO added emphasis for certified companies to prove understanding of their organization and the interdependencies with external stakeholders. I expect this emphasis will help those mired in average performance take a positive step forward. But this industry change will need time to mature before the benefits come to full fruition.

When companies don't consider this external environment and the full context of their organization, they're failing to consider all the forces relevant to their current state. It's impossible to develop a valid strategic direction without fully appreciating this context. This again requires systems thinking. The strongest leaders understand the relation of their company to both the local and world community.

Few companies now operate insular and independent of other entities. Whether we like it or not, the world is now interconnected and will continue to become more so with increased velocity. A by-product of this connectedness is that our companies now have multiple interested parties. The economic fall-out from the coronavirus pandemic helped many of us realize the extent of this connectedness. Our new reality is yet another reason that underscores the importance of systems thinking.

A company's focus, inward or outward, dictates its internal investment and how it allocates internal funds, to include those for research and development. But other factors also influence these decisions, to include the organizational life cycle and the relative focus on the customer.

There's no single right answer for approaching this investment. But there can be a wrong answer.

At times, the right answer may be to maximize innovation and development of new products and services using principles from the CVF *create* quadrant. Other times, the best answer may be to focus on production efficiency to increase profits for future investment through principles inherent to the framework's *control* quadrant.

Leadership makes the decision based upon product life cycles within the marketspace. While there's no single right answer, failing to make the right decision within the circumstances will directly affect whether a company moves closer to, or further from, excellence.

AN EXAMPLE OF EXCELLENCE

Throughout this work, I've provided specific examples that fell short of excellence. I've shared these in the spirit of transparency, primarily for their learning value. Excellence is a rare state, few organizations achieve it, and even fewer can maintain it.

We learn more from our failures. But then again, moving far beyond average, even if falling short of excellence, shouldn't necessarily be considered a failure. We shouldn't discount the positive value of any movement that gets us closer to the target.

My career has been one of continual movement. I've had the pleasure to be associated with several organizations within the public and private sectors that have achieved excellence.

Over the last 30 years, I've worked with quite a few major corporations and different government agencies. Each opportunity allowed me to engage as a member of some very good organizations. Some had already achieved excellence or were very close to doing so. And some had to make fundamental changes before moving forward to this sought-after state.

My early drafts for this work included several examples of organizations that achieved excellence. I wrote about roles ranging from my first job in college, delivering pizzas at Domino's, to later roles helping deliver high-reliable satellite systems. But in the interest of keeping focus on learning through mistakes, I've limited discussion here to a single example. An example that departs from private industry, which has been the focus for most of this book.

I want to provide a single abbreviated example of my journey to excellence. It was one that I participated in from the other side of the world.

I served an exchange tour with the Royal Australian Air Force (RAAF) from 1999 to 2001. My role was to manage maintenance and flight-line operations for a 21 plane Australian F/A-18 squadron in Williamtown, New South Wales.

The day I joined the unit, less than half the planes were airworthy. Not one of them was combat-ready. The RAAF men and women were proud people, but a sense of complacency dominated the culture. Fixed-winged RAAF aircraft hadn't seen combat since the Korean War. The daily target for serviceable aircraft was ten or less than 50 percent readiness. Activity-based goals drove the measurement for combat readiness. Success meant completing 100 percent of the inspections, regardless of results.

The "way things get done around here" was permeated by a lack of urgency. Labor times to complete maintenance actions were twice as high as similar US units. As an example, RAAF mechanics would take more than two hours to replace an aircraft generator. I was used to it taking less than 60 minutes.

We started changing everything my second day.

We increased the daily readiness target to 15 aircraft. Within six months, we consistently met this new target. The combat readiness checks were changed to an outcome-based goal and often reported dismal results. But changes were implemented and within the year were regularly exceeding 90 percent fully mission-capable.

Our Commanding Officer, Geoff Brown, was a beloved man and a strong leader. A year into our transformation, he advised of his planned retirement from service. The traditional retirement send-off is a large fly-over for the officer's final flight.

I challenged the maintenance team with a breakthrough goal of having 20 of our 21 aircraft for the fly-over. At first, they thought this to be impossible. But as we began to approach the goal, they challenged me back and decided to try and have all 21 aircraft participate. The squadron hadn't had all 21 aircraft serviceable in the last 20 years.

The day of the fly-over came, and 21 RAAF pilots "walked" to 21 combat-ready F/A-18 aircraft. During the start-up routine, one of the planes experienced a failed generator. I thought we were doomed. But a team of mechanics responded. With the pilot still in the cockpit, they replaced the generator in 15 minutes. Thirty minutes later, a 21-plane formation screamed above RAAF Base Williamtown, providing an honorable send-off for Wing Commander Brown.

Several months later, Geoff Brown was retired and selling real estate on Australia's Gold Coast. I was back in the States, assigned to the Commander, Naval Air Forces, Atlantic Fleet. And then 19 terrorists hijacked four planes bringing their war to America and the world.

Geoff Brown came out of retirement and rose through the ranks to eventually lead the entire RAAF as Chief of Air Force. And that squadron from Williamtown, it deployed a contingent of fully combat-ready aircraft, of operationally excellent aircraft, as it allied with America in the Global War on Terrorism.

Part V

Why These Things Matter

Urban legend tells of an experiment on rhesus monkeys that goes something like this.

A scientist places five monkeys in a cage. He puts a ladder in the middle of the cage and hangs some bananas from the ceiling. Within minutes, one of the monkeys decides to climb the ladder. He doesn't get far. The scientist uses a firehose to blast the monkey with a powerful spray. He soaks the monkey and his four friends for several long minutes. Then the punishment ends.

The monkeys aren't happy.

Soon they forget about the water and once again, eye the bananas. A different monkey attempts to climb the ladder. The water punishment returns. The monkey is knocked to the ground and each monkey is again soaked. Chaos returns to the cage. After making his point, the scientist withdraws his punishment and the monkeys eventually calm down.

Then a third monkey draws on his courage and goes for the bananas. But the pattern has revealed itself.

As soon as his foot hits the ladder, the other four pummel him to the ground. They beat him without mercy. The scientist watches but doesn't use his hose. He doesn't need to. The monkeys learned to enforce desired behavior within their group.

None of the monkeys ever again attempt to climb the ladder.

After a certain period, the scientist replaces one of the monkeys. The new monkey sees the bananas and soon ascends the ladder. But the other monkeys enforce their rules. They drag him from the ladder and proceed to teach him why this isn't acceptable behavior. He doesn't know why he was beaten, but he also never again tries to get the bananas.

The cycle continues with the scientist replacing each original monkey, one by one. Each new monkey soon attempts to climb the ladder. And each time the other monkeys respond with violence. Once beaten, a monkey never again tries to get the bananas.

All five original monkeys are eventually replaced. None remaining has felt the spray of the hose. Time passes and yet the monkeys don't try to get the bananas. The scientist is nowhere to be seen.

Yet the monkeys ignore the bananas. They carry on with their day, aware of the bananas, but unwilling to climb the ladder.

At this point, they don't know why they don't do so.

They only know this is how they've always done it.

12

Application

Our world *is* changing—some say changing too fast. Much of this confronts our core beliefs, how we see the world. And some if it challenges our beliefs in the integrity of business. We observed isolated cases of price gouging and profiteering during the coronavirus pandemic. And prior to that, we've observed the realities of high-profile greed and unethical behavior in business.

But we have hope for moving beyond this cynicism.

Signs indicate a growing movement to restore emphasis on ethical behavior. Nearly 200 of America's most influential CEOs recently acknowledge this reality. They agreed in a formal mission statement that the larger societal role of corporations is to help create a life of meaning and dignity. Professional organizations are developing pledges confirming a commitment to work by a code of ethics. And values-based leaders are emphasizing respect for the individual, adhering to democratic principles, and engendering trust and a renewed commitment.

Our companies and marketspaces *are* changing.

What used to be trivial is now important and vice versa. Globalization, technology, sustainability, and values each help define a company's triple bottom line. Ignoring changes in these areas leads to diminishing returns—and eventual failure.

Our companies are struggling with ways to become more competitive, to reduce costs, and to chase unobtanium in their never-ending pursuit to do more with less. But to survive, this focus on efficiency must not come at the expense of innovation, agility, and moving fast.

As the coronavirus spread across the world, ventilator availability quickly hit critical mass. Companies that were making cars and vacuum cleaners in February were making ventilators in March. One company even completed a design and began production within ten days. We haven't seen adaptability and responsiveness like this since World War II. But challenging times drive innovation. Our overwhelming need drove rapid transformation. And the most forward-leaning companies responded.

Outside of this crisis, our legacy attempts to transform businesses have been myopic. They placed too much emphasis on a singular approach, such as focusing on Lean or Six Sigma. These approaches missed the broader changes affecting how businesses are now succeeding. Innovation and agility are now more valued than efficiency, technical precision, and waste reduction. And as we move forward, rapid adaptability and resilience will become the preferential traits.

Taking definitive steps towards Operational Excellence, as discussed throughout this book, provides the foundation to optimize costs while embracing efficiency, innovation, agility, and adaptability. And an operationally excellent company will be a resilient company.

This world that we live in requires new ideas. Classical management approaches will no longer deliver the goals we seek. We need a new approach to management—one that enables us to achieve excellence.

When we approach these challenges through values-based leadership and by taking a systems approach, we can change the course of work. And in return, we can realize greater performance while improving the circumstances for those accomplishing the work.

COST, PRICE, AND VALUE

We need to revisit a company's purpose as viewed from its own perspective. When a company believes its purpose is to return shareholder value through making more money, it focuses on *price* and *profit*. This is not the path for those pursuing excellence.

Companies pursuing excellence focus on their own *cost* and *value* delivered to the customer.

When cost and value are not the focus of control, price is viewed as a lever that can be increased to maintain profit margin. Such is the state of a traditional market economy made up of companies mired in average performance.

There are different schools of thought here relative to cost, price, and value that we need to consider.

Classically trained managers prefer the traditional *cost-plus view of price*. It's the approach typically employed by most American companies. Under this model, price is established as the sum of total costs, which include fixed and variable costs, plus profit, mathematically represented as:

$$\text{Price} = \left[\text{Fixed Costs} + \text{Variable Costs}\right] + \text{Profit}$$

Many factors go into establishing price, which under this model determines how much profit to charge. Variables associated with the product and marketspace help determine the pricing strategy. But the marketspace remains the final authority for determining how much it is willing to pay.

While there may be casual efforts to reduce fixed and variable costs, they're not a genuine concern. Through the economies involved, costs gradually increase. As the product and marketspace mature, profits eventually erode to the point that the product is no longer viable. The product faces termination once cost exceeds the marketspace price tolerance.

The cycle can refresh if the company introduces product improvements through innovation or a competitor rebirths the product with new features.

Figure 12.1 displays the typical pattern for product life cycles under this model. An initial life cycle for a product can vary from months to years to decades. Examples of products following this model are cell phones. Or most everything procured by the US government under legacy acquisition strategies.

But there is a model that has historically worked better—one with roots in Lean. This model takes a *process view of cost* and assumes there are many other levers at our disposal, each of them focused on the cost of the

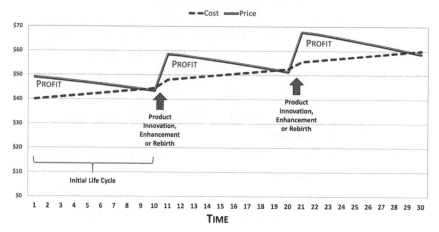

FIGURE 12.1

Cost-plus view of price.

process. Such an approach has historically been pursued by operationally excellent companies that continually seek to lower operating costs.

Lean thinking operates with a mindset that processes generate cost. This drives the perspective that improving process is the surest way to reduce cost. Under this model, profit is the remaining element once costs are reduced through all possible means and subtracted from the price the marketspace is willing to pay. But under this customer-focused approach, as costs are reduced, the price is also reduced while profits remain relatively constant.

With the mindset that processes generate cost, we assess cost with an approach more detailed than just fixed and variable. There are value-added costs, such as the actual production effort. There are wastes, referred to in Lean speak as *muda*, classified as Type 1 (necessary but non-value-added) and Type 2 (unnecessary and non-value-added). We seek to optimize Type 1 and eliminate Type 2 waste. The two other cost drivers are referred to as *mura*, the workflow unevenness, and *muri*, the overburdening of the system. We represent this mathematically as follows:

$$\text{Profit} = \text{Price} - \big[\text{Valued-added Costs} + \text{Waste}(\text{Type1\&2})$$

$$+ \text{Unevenness} + \text{Overburdening}\big]$$

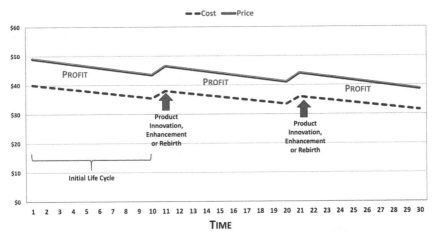

FIGURE 12.2

Process view of cost.

This model provides more levers to pull as we seek to reduce costs. Our discussion on the cost of quality (CoQ) in Chapter 10 highlighted opportunities to manage these cost reductions. But many companies won't take this approach. They avoid it because doing so requires senior leaders to pay attention to things they prefer not to focus on, namely process and causation.

Under this model, we maintain a focused and continual effort to reduce costs. Figure 12.2 displays the typical pattern for product life cycles under this model.

As recent events have taught us all too well, efforts to reduce costs must be tempered against what provides the lowest risk for the highest sustainable return. We must always seek to tactically control costs. But we also must be sure to provide the greatest value at the lowest risk.

While this *process view of cost* is preferred to the *cost-plus view of price*, it may not be the preferred model that we'll need to move towards excellence in our new world. Focusing on price and expecting the customer to make up for it by paying inflated profit margins will remain a recipe for continued average performance. But on the other side of that coin, focusing on extreme cost reductions has proven to weaken our systems through a heavy reliance on over-extended supply chains.

The coronavirus disruption brought many companies to a standstill. In hindsight, some actions taken to reduce costs by outsourcing across the globe resulted in degraded performance and the inability to provide products when needed. This would be the definition of poor value and therefore something that we must alter going forward.

Our new model must continue to focus on reducing costs. But it must not do so through a system that presents increased risk against serving the customer. Value then becomes the driving factor we seek to fulfill so that we achieve not the highest profits but the highest optimized *sustained* profits.

ANALYTICS

Six years ago, I wrote that information is becoming king. Its pre-ordained destiny has been realized. Information is now similar to an economic asset, like currency or gold. Less than ten years ago, it was fashionable to cite more information is produced in one year than was produced in the last five thousand years. That data production *rate* is now doubling every two years.

More than 20 years ago, before digital transformation and this idea of data science was a concept, Bill Gates foresaw our current state in his 1999 book, *Business @ the Speed of Thought*, where he wrote:

> The most meaningful way to differentiate your company from your competition, the best way to put distance between you and the crowd, is to do an outstanding job with information... How you gather, manage, and use information will determine whether you win or lose.

This section will not attempt to explain or provide solutions for the continuing digital transformation. I've instead chosen to discuss the people and the structures associated with analytics that must be enhanced to help move our companies towards excellence.

As business becomes increasingly more complex and information becomes a prime commodity, the effectiveness that we process information establishes our organizational effectiveness. Companies need experts, or even masters, that specialize in the collection, analysis, and synthesis of data through a business intelligence system that allows managers to make timely and effective data-driven decisions.

Having data solves part of the problem. Integrating this data within a business intelligence system solves much of the remainder. But data transformed into information is useless if we don't manage it as knowledge.

Managing this information means that we apply new ways of thinking, to include systems thinking, design thinking, divergent thinking, and both/and thinking. The problems we face today were created with old ways of thinking. New ways of thinking will be required to solve the complex problems that make up our new world.

We're seeking to move beyond *descriptive analytics* limited to hindsight and *diagnostic analytics* that provide insight into why things happened. We want to get to where we aggregate data and shape it into knowledge so we can make better data-driven decisions to *predict* what will happen. And if we are exceptionally good, we'll eventually move towards *prescriptive analytics* that provide foresight so that we can influence what happens.

Central to this effort will be our analysts.

Some analysts, those people tasked with analyzing data and making recommendations, have an identity crisis. They believe themselves to be like meteorologists, responsible for only reporting what they see. They fail to dive deeper and find out why something is, and to understand the issue at its root prior to making a recommendation. This is usually because we haven't empowered them to be more.

We should encourage our analysts to go beyond merely reporting data. We should expect them to characterize the associated causes. By taking this extra step, those accountable for making data-driven decisions *will* make better decisions.

Our analysts are force multipliers that can make others around them better. They give us another example where 1 + 1 can equal more than 2. And most importantly, they can be stabilizing forces that provide data to help us answer questions that didn't exist several months ago.

We previously discussed job enlargement and job enrichment. We can benefit by expanding the analyst role through both concepts. Expansion through job enlargement could entail analysts actively participating in the review of processes that generate data. And job enrichment could include having them participate in management reviews to increase their understanding of how the data they collect, analyze, and process is used to make improved management decisions.

Just before taking over organizations I knew to be struggling, I've often provided my leadership philosophy to those I was about to manage. Each time, I emphasized the importance of data and those in a data analyst role. I'm convinced this precursor move helped ensure success in each of these challenging positions.

But merely stating importance without following through with support achieves nothing. We need to change the expectations placed upon analysts. People *will* respond when we expect more from them. But they may need additional training to include formal instruction in systems thinking, synthesis, and root cause analysis. Once provided additional training and empowered to add more value, they'll become force multipliers for our companies.

These are simple things. They're also uncommon things. And that's the thing about excellence, it's uncommon by definition.

Our organizations have different layers of structure for execution and management that allow them to assess information, determine what it means, and then act. Our understanding of risk is baked into and inextricable from this process. And within the different levels of the organization, there are different expectations for managing the patterns of information and the inherent risk.

Let's consider an example within the operations function for a typical large manufacturer, where the employees range from machine operators up through the vice president of operations.

The machine operators are exposed to tactical product and process information as they build the company's products. They sometimes encounter situations outside of expectations that require risk-based decisions. Their roles are typically highly structured, and expectations are emplaced that limit risk exposure through boundaries that define what levels of risk they can assume.

The manager supervising the operators is afforded more decision leeway. The operators raise up issues where the decision is outside their authority. The manager can choose to make a risk-based decision with the available information or seek counsel up the chain, from the director of manufacturing. The director can assume more risk than the manager and can facilitate the continued product movement, or if outside his level of authority, can pass the information up to the vice president of operations.

As a senior executive, the vice president is afforded significantly more authority and can assume greater risk to keep the production line moving. He can assess the situation and make the decision, or in rare cases, he can pass the information to the president for a final decision.

In each of these transactions, the act of deciding can be a decision to do nothing. This inaction withholds information and knowledge up the chain for further assessment and awareness. While information may be king, knowledge is power.

This behavior can result in patterns of information that are not effectively assessed. Information is either lost or not used at the right level to make informed decisions needed to manage the company.

In *The Challenger Launch Decision*, Diane Vaughan referred to this as *structural secrecy*. This structural secrecy can undermine our need to know and interpret information critical to the business. The volume of information available to our employees is ever-increasing. Through establishing open communication channels and fostering an environment based upon trust, we can avoid what NASA didn't and that ultimately contributed to the *Challenger* disaster.

Several years ago, Jim was a statistician that led my Operational Excellence team. His talents with numbers were impressive. And he was a force multiplier. Our Quality group was superb at identifying issues, no matter how remote or potentially insignificant. They once identified a latent defect in an engine bearing that could affect thousands of delivered products. The information was openly shared up the chain and quickly made it to me, as the vice president of operations.

Jim conducted a thorough failure mode and effects analysis showing probabilities for impact and likelihood of occurrence. I quickly shared his data with the president. The likelihood for failure was extremely remote, but if occurring, the consequences would be catastrophic. Considering this, and that products were already delivered, the information flow extended even beyond the president. We briefed the customer and openly shared Jim's data. This was not only the right thing to do, but through our transparency, we gained a noted degree of trust from the customer.

Jim is now a semi-retired consultant. The other day I saw one of his most recent studies. He re-calculated the mortality rates for the coronavirus based upon the latest available data. The subject here is very different from analyzing mechanical failures. The importance and gravity cannot be compared. But the underlying importance of data is underscored. Not having accurate data places leaders in a position where they either don't make a decision when required or they make the wrong decision.

Jim also helped me understand the importance of the assumptions around our data. These frame the context of our data. If the assumptions prove to be wrong, then our information is not reliable. We discussed the importance of assumptions in problem-solving. They are just as important for our analysis of data. We must always try to validate our assumptions to confirm the reliability of the data.

A company that desires to move beyond average embraces a culture of transparency—one that shares good and bad news with equal vigor. Such a company has people and information systems in place to understand this data, transform it into reliable information, and use this information as knowledge to improve our understanding of things.

MEASURING PERFORMANCE

Surely most companies measure performance. Those certified to the most common Quality Management System (QMS), ISO 9001, are obliged to do so to maintain conformance. But we're looking to move beyond just conformance. And in doing so, some adjustments may be necessary for how we measure performance. The most important consideration here is *what* we measure. Metrics, goals, and objectives measure and report on different things and have different purposes.

Earlier in our values discussion, we clarified that a metric is like a value in that it's a comparison of one thing to another. A metric by itself doesn't determine goodness, rather, a metric helps us measure performance compared against a known standard. And there has historically been but one purpose for these metrics: to modify behavior.

The premise for this entire book has been that to achieve excellence, we must shift our focus to changing the way people think. We don't want them to be satisfied with average conforming behavior. We want them to realize that different performance, breakthrough performance, is indeed possible. And we want our metrics to reflect this desired new behavior. At this fundamental level, metrics are used to measure our success towards getting people to think differently.

The metrics tied to key business processes form our Key Performance Indicators, or KPIs. These KPIs provide management insight into performance areas that impact business-level objectives.

Readers of this work are well versed in metrics and the importance of performance measurement. We all get and deeply understand that what gets measured, improves. Our measurement systems, and what we choose to measure, will be critical to help us move towards excellence. Rather than reinforce these things that are evident, I'm going to quickly highlight three considerations critical to include within our measurement approach.

The first consideration occurs before we make any measurement or design any system to collect data. We must start with the end in mind. General familiarity with this phrase may lead some to think I've just mastered the obvious. Reality indicates otherwise.

I've seen countless measurement systems doomed to mediocrity from their beginning. They were designed without adequate consideration for how the data would be used to make better decisions. At the onset of any project, initiative, or system, we must be intentional to pre-define our expected measures of effectiveness. Not doing so places far too much trust in luck and chance to deliver expected results.

The second consideration is a cultural factor and precursor to any improvement. The organization, starting with top management, must be transparent about openly sharing data needed to make improvements. This transparency is often absent where it's required most. Here again, we see *structural secrecy* play a part. This is especially true in those companies where business units "compete" against one another for favor and larger bonuses.

And considering bonuses, the compensation system is a great lever to stimulate transparency. Sub-optimized performance shouldn't be rewarded when the greater good of the enterprise isn't served. Allocation of management bonuses to consider the "whole" performance is a wonderful way to mitigate sub-optimization and its underlying lack of transparency.

The final consideration for our measurement approach relates to transparency and reviewing performance against breakthrough goals. It's important to respond appropriately without over-reacting to performance that fails to meet stretch goals needed to achieve breakthrough performance.

We should again remember how a parent teaches their child to ride a bike—steady encouragement and coaching, without over-reacting to setbacks. This same approach will ultimately bring us the results we seek. But we shouldn't ignore performance that doesn't meet the target without a valid countermeasure. This is the essence of accountability and our responsibility as leaders.

In less mature or trusting organizations, expectation for this accountability may appear to some as "being put on the spot." But that is exactly where we want them. We want to learn from them—the obstacles and impediments they are facing so that we as leaders can help them achieve their goals. When we do this, and do this with transparency and honesty, we will take a giant step towards achieving excellence.

MANAGEMENT SYSTEMS

A common definition for a management system is a set of policies, processes, and procedures used by an organization to help fulfill the tasks required to achieve its objectives. If we consider the American government as our organization, then the Preamble establishes the six objectives of government and the Constitution is the management system.

I started with the government as its regulation has become progressively more active, and intrusive, into business. Companies are being forced to create new organizations and processes as management systems to ensure continued compliance in this increasingly regulatory environment.

But the government isn't the only external entity driving the need for these management systems. Our customers and even society indirectly levy us to emplace these systems.

We previously discussed the increasing importance to adjust our focus outward to consider the entire context of the organization. Having this systems perspective, we can see the impact society can have on our companies when they don't like something about us. The speed at which social media transmits information about us and our companies must now be taken into full consideration.

A couple of years ago, a major US airline faced a public relations nightmare after a 69-year-old man refused to give up his ticketed seat. He was forcibly drug off the plane. Social media instantly exploded, and the public quickly demonized the airline. The government's initial response was of course to threaten new regulations. The root of the problem traced to the airline's practice of overbooking flights. While I don't have personal insight into their final corrective actions, I'm willing to bet there's another management system now in place to manage this process.

Our companies typically have numerous management systems that help ensure compliance to regulations and conformance to standards. Examples include management systems for environmental requirements, occupational safety and health requirements, accounting system requirements, and of course, quality requirements. There are many others.

As of April 2020, ISO identifies 47 different management system standards to which organizations can claim conformance and seek certification. These management systems and their self-generated requirements placed on the organization increase as a company grows and becomes more complex.

Each management system creates another layer of bureaucracy and complexity. And unfortunately, each system tends to generate its own requirements for internal auditing, metrics, goals, risk management, and training.

The owner of each system inherently argues for their importance. This tends to increase resources needed for execution year over year. While the owners may have good intent, managing these systems as individual entities invariably leads to sub-optimization. And it comes with a cost in the form of increased overhead and redundancy that continually decrease efficiency across the enterprise.

The new world we're now facing will soon provide justifications for yet even more management systems. As an example, before the pandemic, many companies had business continuity plans that helped them respond to the crisis. Others did not, and they struggled.

It shouldn't surprise that one of the 47 management systems ISO establishes certification standards for includes a Business Continuity Management System. The importance of such a system should be obvious, especially now. However, we must have an intentional plan for responding to this growing requirement for an ever-increasing number of management systems.

Another example is the requirement to establish a new complex management system driven by increased government regulation. There are new requirements companies must emplace to manage cybersecurity when doing business with the Department of Defense (DoD). The Cybersecurity Maturity Model Certification (CMMC) required by the DoD will require companies to have increasing levels of cybersecurity certification starting in 2020.

Under CMMC, companies will need external parties to conduct compliance audits and assess risk. Those doing business with the DoD will need to create additional internal auditing plans and develop new metrics and training programs, thereby adding even more complexity and overhead to the organization.

This is one example. There are many others. And surely in the future, there will be more requirements levied by the government and influenced by society. Our companies may soon have to deal with the continued growth of social media and the ongoing digital transformation by creating even more management systems. If we continue our current path, each new management system will be sub-optimized and add another layer of complexity and inefficiency to the organization.

More management systems simply lead to more processes that we need to control. These processes become more difficult to manage as they grow and become more complex. On the near extreme, this results in poor execution, loss of process control, and degraded business performance. On the far extreme, it results in unfettered friction, victimhood, poor decision-making, and normalized deviance.

Several times throughout this book, I've used laws from physics to help explain organizational behavior.

Discussing this growth and complexity of management systems presents another such opportunity.

Taking liberties with the second law of thermodynamics, we know that things trend towards disorder and that within any closed system, net chaos can never be reduced. Through analogy, we shouldn't be surprised by the overall disorder produced by these disparate management systems. And the greater the number of these independent and closed systems, the higher the likelihood for disorder in the form of redundancy, bureaucracy, and increased overhead needed to maintain them year over year.

But there is another solution.

There's a growing trend among forward-leaning companies to replace their different management systems with a consolidated Business Management System (BMS). Doing so requires more than simple procedural consolidation. This is more than a mapping exercise and requires systems thinking to account for the various interdependencies. It will require intentional action to eliminate sub-optimization while optimizing internal processes needed to ensure conformance and compliance.

The actions to create a BMS take work. Sometimes lots of administrative work. But this is one administrative task where the juice is worth the squeeze.

A consolidated BMS is a system of interdependent tools for strategic planning and tactical implementation of policies, processes, and procedures. The BMS facilitates the efficient development, deployment, and execution of business plans and strategies. The purpose of a BMS is to ensure effective conformance to industry standards and efficient compliance to regulatory requirements. It is literally the high-level playbook for how the business is managed.

As expected, consultancies now exist that specialize in converting different management systems into a consolidated BMS. But as I've mentioned before, companies must be careful when outsourcing their eyes. Management systems often contain the secret sauce of our companies. While outsiders are fine for bringing in best practices, these outsiders weren't the ones that created the secret sauce.

The QMS can serve as the base of an integrated BMS. But to clarify, the intent isn't to create yet another management system but to replace the QMS and other subordinate management systems. The new system enables opportunities to reduce chaos driven from redundancies and inefficiencies. And replacing the QMS with a BMS doesn't reduce the importance of quality within the company; it enhances quality and raises it to a level where senior leadership maintain direct ownership. The BMS is owned and championed by top management.

If a company's QMS is certified to one of the ISO family of standards, then the QMS is based upon the seven Quality Management Principles discussed in Chapter 1. That's a good start to expand our intent beyond average performance. Most of us want more, especially if we've read to this point in the book.

Approaching the problem through the lens of Operational Excellence provides an enhanced solution. These Operational Excellence concepts provide us the best solution for constructing an integrated BMS. The result will be a single management system that provides an integrated approach to internal auditing, metrics, performance measurement, continual improvement, process governance, and training.

The characteristics and mindsets discussed throughout this book can help a company establish a BMS that will directly assist in the pursuit of excellence. The most effective BMS will be designed around these Operational Excellence principles. It could also incorporate elements from the Baldrige Excellence criteria and the ISO Quality Management Principles. It should be a management system that reflects these proven practices and is fully integrated with the overall business planning cycle.

We're seeking to move beyond average. This will require a new foundation. We establish this foundation by implementing an integrated business execution system—a BMS that aligns strategies and effectively integrates the people, processes, and products.

CONCLUSION

Part I of this work opened with a reminder from King Solomon that there's nothing new. But times are changing. We must remove those vestiges from the past that hold our companies back from achieving more, from achieving excellence. The magnitude of the past will always be increasing. As Marshall Goldsmith advised in his review of this work, clinging to the past keeps us from moving towards excellence. While we must never assume the past can be ignored, we can be intentional and create a new state for the present and the future—a state based upon the principles of excellence.

Part II discussed those things in our organizations that we don't see or don't necessarily appreciate for their importance. But they often drive our ability to achieve excellence.

Part III then assessed those things we do see, namely, our people, processes, and products and their importance to our pursuit of excellence.

Part IV addressed the things the customer sees, the things that affect their experience, and the reasons for our company's existence.

And finally, Part V discussed why these things matter—application for many of our previous discussions coalesced on our journey to excellence.

This thing called excellence is an elusive and continuing journey. It is not a point destination. And it's not a plaque or certificate our companies are awarded to hang on the wall.

When Vince Lombardi challenged his team to "catch excellence," there wasn't any misunderstanding that the work would end there. Holding onto excellence requires work, hard work. Companies seeking to raise their performance to this level willingly agree to remain in a constant state of pursuit.

We can think of excellence as a state of mind—a way of thinking, a prevailing attitude, a mindset—that encompasses the principles discussed throughout this book.

Joseph Paris, author of this book's Foreword, describes Operational Excellence as a "state of readiness." Companies that manage to continually operate in this state of excellence are in rarified air. Constant subtle and overt forces attempt to return our organizations to the equilibrium of average performance. These can be driven through comfort with the achievements realized or a desire to harvest the benefits of superior performance.

The natural state of a company is not one of excellence. It will require as much energy to maintain this state as it did to achieve it in the first place. But that is a battle that will always be worth fighting. I predict this pursuit of excellence—of Operational Excellence—can help frame our recovery from the current crisis and help our companies become more resilient. I believe this situation will transform our companies into something stronger and better than they were before.

And although individuals, including myself, have obtained certifications in excellence, I caution those with the power to do so *not* to establish organizational certifications in excellence. Organizational certifications to meet certain standards of performance are fine in other areas but not in excellence. The decision to pursue excellence needs to be one that is not customer-driven or mandatory in any way.

This decision to pursue excellence must come about because top leadership supports and believes in the idea. Excellence is only achievable through an honest intent to pursue it by those that believe in it. Any attempt to standardize excellence works against the defining characteristics of what it means to be excellent. There will always be a need and room for average performance. The laws of statistics will remain valid in the future.

But many of us won't be satisfied with average performance. We are the ones who will continue to pursue excellence.

Epilogue

The ideas discussed throughout this book, of Operational Excellence, provide concepts for our companies to move beyond average and towards excellent performance. Each idea introduced included discussion of its underlying importance to Operational Excellence.

And while few of these ideas were discussed in full detail, there was a basic theme of *values-based leadership* and *systems thinking* weaved into each discussion. I don't believe it's possible to attain this state of excellence without these characteristics.

Companies may be able to become quite good, but they won't achieve excellence in performance if they do not embrace these concepts.

The complexity and new realities of our world require that we approach organizational life from a systems perspective. Not doing so will always fail to deliver the whole solution needed within a complex environment. And not embracing values-based leadership will always result in people not performing to their highest potential. We can develop perfect plans and strategies, but without people motivated and inspired to execute them, our efforts will not sustain.

This book has been about leadership. And not just any kind of leadership. I haven't emphasized the concept with a name to this point. But the most favorable leadership for companies pursuing excellence is leadership of a servant nature.

Robert Greenleaf brought this notion of servant leadership to our community with his 1970 essay, *The Servant as Leader*. In this work, Greenleaf describes servant leadership through a series of questions where he queries the basis of an individual's intent. The essence of the philosophy is the belief that a leader must put others first and help people develop to perform to their full potential. His work now serves as the foundation for the advancement, understanding, and application of these concepts. But Greenleaf certainly didn't invent the philosophy.

Servant leadership is timeless. Human history reveals its evidence from our beginning. We see it documented in the writings of the Bible, the teachings of Buddha, and the principles of ancient Chinese philosophers.

This concept of servant leadership is simple. It's simple, yet in our world with its focus on things as they have become, it can seem complex. But the more we come to understand the concept, the more we realize it's anything but complex.

Remember that I believe words are very important. One way to better understand servant leadership is to study the words that embody the essence of the idea. Larry Spears, previous director for the Greenleaf Center for Servant Leadership, identified characteristics common to servant leaders. The central meanings behind these ideas help frame the philosophy. The concepts Spears identifies as vital to a servant leader's development include:

Listening	Persuasion
Empathy	Foresight
Healing	Conceptualization
Awareness	Stewardship
Commitment to the growth of people	Building community

I would also add humility, authenticity, and transparency to this list. And although not intended as a complete list, a leader's commitment to these types of characteristics affects their positive impact on others. A dedicated commitment to these concepts across the organization helps improve the overall quality of organizational life.

In the book *Insights on Leadership*, Steven Covey wrote of servant leadership as a principle, a natural law. Covey explains having our "social value systems and personal habits aligned with this ennobling principle is one of the great challenges of our lives." In the same book, Ken Blanchard helps clarify the servant leader role through the hierarchical paradox and inverted organizational pyramid. Here, employees don't work for the leader, the leader works for the employees. Finally, those familiar with Jim Collins will note many of the characteristics of a *Level 5 Leader* closely correlate to servant leadership.

Some companies have embraced servant-based leadership and outperformed their peers. But these remain the exception. Few companies honestly incorporate these fundamentals with how they run their business.

Similarly, some companies have taken the bold steps to become operationally excellent. These again are the rare exception. But they don't have to be.

Through embracing the concepts discussed in this book, all sizes of companies can achieve excellent results. Those doing so don't have to be the rare exception. This is the path many of us desire. But these ideas to transform our businesses must be championed at the very top and then embraced by those expected to affect the change.

The core theories forming the foundation for this work are not new concepts. They are proven ideas. But they are ideas that previously haven't been integrated into a holistic solution.

At no point did I present these ideas and this approach to leadership as something new. On the contrary, if anything has remained constant throughout human history, it's the basic tenants of what lies at the heart of positive and effective relationships and human interactions. This is the essence of leadership. The characteristics of mercy, kindness, humility, gentleness, patience, forgiveness, dignity, trust, and honesty have remained the relationship goals for humanity. These are the things we seek to be.

No matter how much the world changes, or what the make-up or timing is of the next crisis, we need to be leaders. We need to be the leaders that help ensure these foundational characteristics remain as the driving energy behind our sought-after solutions.

Notes

CHAPTER 1

See *http://businessexcellence.org/* for more information.

The ASQ definitions for *Excellence* and *Organizational Excellence* are used with permission and are available at *https://asq.org/*.

The seven ISO Quality Management Principles as published in International Organization for Standardization, *Quality Management Principles*. Geneva, Switzerland, 2015.

Emiliani quote reprinted with permission from Bob Emiliani, *The Triumph of Classical Management over Lean Management: How Tradition Prevails and What to do about It*. Cubic LLC, South Kingstown, RI 2018, p. 275.

John Krafcik, "Triumph of the Lean Production System." *Sloan Management Review*, Vol. 30, No. 1 (1988): pp. 41–52.

Lewin's *Change* and *Force Field Models* adapted from concepts identified in Kurt Lewin, "Frontiers in Group Dynamics." *Human Relations*, Vol. 1, No. 5 (1947): pp. 5–41.

PART II

Christopher F. Chabris and Daniel J. Simons, *The Invisible Gorilla: And Other Ways Our Intuitions Deceive Us*. Crown, New York, 2010.

CHAPTER 2

Robert E. Quinn and John Rohrbaugh, "A Spatial Model of Effectiveness Criteria: Towards a Competing Values Approach to Organizational Analysis." *Management Science*, Vol. 29, No. 3 (1983): pp. 363–377.

Kim S. Cameron and Robert E. Quinn, *Diagnosing and Changing Organizational Culture: Based on the Competing Values Framework.* 3rd ed. Jossey-Bass, San Francisco, 2011.

CHAPTER 3

Schein's definition reprinted with permission as published in Edgar H. Schein with Peter Schein, *Organizational Culture and Leadership.* 5th ed. Jossey-Bass, San Francisco, 2016.

Learning concepts obtained from ideas established in Martin M. Broadwell, "Teaching for Learning (XVI.)." *The Gospel Guardian*, Vol. 20, No. 41 (1969): p. 1-3a.

Roger Dooley, *Friction: The Untapped Force That Can Be Your Most Powerful Advantage.* McGraw-Hill, New York, 2019.

Taiichi Ohno, *Toyota Production System – Beyond Large-Scale Production.* Productivity Press, Portland, OR, 1988.

Diane Vaughan, *The Challenger Launch Decision: Risky Technology, Culture and Deviance at NASA.* University Press, Chicago, 1996.

Roger C. Mayer, James H. Davis and F. David Schoorman. "An Integrative Model of Organizational Trust." *Academy of Management Review,* Vol. 20, No. 3 (1995): pp. 709–734.

Peter Block. *Stewardship: Choosing Service Over Self Interest.* Berrett-Koehler, San Francisco, 1993.

CHAPTER 4

Marcus Buckingham and Curt Coffman. *First, Break All the Rules: What the World's Greatest Managers Do Differently*. New York, NY: Simon & Schuster, 1999.

Paul Hersey and Ken Blanchard. *Management of Organizational Behavior; Utilizing Human Resources*. Englewood Cliffs, NJ: Prentice-Hall, 1969.

Management skills model of Figure 4.1 adapted from concepts originally published in Robert Katz, "Skills of an Effective Administrator." *Harvard Business Review*, (1955): pp. 33–42.

Marshall Goldsmith and Mark Reiter. *What Got You Here Won't Get You There: How Successful People Become Even More Successful*. New York, NY: Hyperion, 2007.

Colonel John Boyd's theory behind his OODA loop has been documented in numerous US Defense Department briefs and concept papers to become the common idea generally accepted today.

CHAPTER 6

ISO 9001 Quality Management System. International Organization for Standardization. Geneva, 2015.

Elbert Hubbard. *A Message to Garcia*. The Roycrofters, East Aurora, NY, 1903. © 1899.

John Krafcik, "Triumph of the Lean Production System." *Sloan Management Review*, Vol. 30, No. 1 (1988): pp. 41–52.

CHAPTER 7

Michael Watkins, *The First 90 Days*. Harvard Business School Press, Boston, 2003.

Nassim Nicholas Taleb. *The Black Swan: The Impact of the Highly Improbable*. Random House, New York, 2007.

Bill Gates. *The Next outbreak? We're not ready*. [Video File] March 2015. Available at *https://www.ted.com/talks/ bill_gates_the_next_ outbreak_we_re_not_ready*.

Vincent C.C. Cheng, Susanna K.P. Lau, Patrick C.Y. Woo, and Kwok Yung Yuen. "Severe Acute Respiratory Syndrome Coronavirus as an Agent of Emerging and Reemerging Infection." *Clinical Microbiology Reviews*, Vol. 20, No. 4 (2007): pp. 660–694.

Nassim Nicholas Taleb. *Antifragile: Things That Gain from Disorder (Incerto)*. Random House, New York, 2012.

See *https://www.washingtonpost.com/business/2020/04/02/boeing-offers-employees-buyouts-us-economy-shudders/*.

Kim W. Chan and Renée Mauborgne. *Blue Ocean Strategy: How to Create Uncontested Market Space and Make the Competition Irrelevant*. Harvard Business School Press, Boston, 2005.

See *https://www.justice.gov/opa/pr/wells-fargo-agrees-pay-3-billion-resolve-criminal-and-civil-investigations-sales-practices*.

PART III

See *https://www.cnbc.com/marcus-lemonis-bio/*.

CHAPTER 8

See *https://news.gallup.com/poll/241649/employee-engagement-rise.aspx*.

Robert E. Quinn. *Deep Change: Discovering the Leader Within*. Jossey-Bass, San Francisco, 1996.

Susan Cain. *Quiet: The Power of Introverts in a World That Can't Stop Talking.* Broadway Books, New York, 2013.

CHAPTER 9

Verlyn Klinkenborg. *Several Short Sentences About Writing.* Vintage Books, New York, 2013.

CHAPTER 10

Sinek is possibly best known for his TED Talk and his discussion of *why*. Simon Sinek. *How great leaders inspire action.* [Video File] Sept 2009. Available at *www.ted.com/talks/simon_sinek_how_great_leaders_inspire_action.*

Jane Chen. "A Warm Embrace that Saves Lives." *C.K. Prahalad's Legacy: Business for Poverty Alleviation.* University of San Diego, Joan B. Kroc Institute for Peace and Justice, San Diego. Lecture. 16 Sept 2011.

Masaaki Imai. KAIZEN: The Key to Japan's Competitive Success. McGraw-Hill, New York, 1986.

PART IV

Elbert Hubbard. *A Message to Garcia.* The Roycrofters, East Aurora, NY, 1903. © 1899.

CHAPTER 11

See *https://qz.com/work/1690439/new-business-roundtable-statement-on-the-purpose-of-companies/.*

CHAPTER 12

Bill Gates. *Business @ the Speed of Thought: Succeeding in the Digital Economy.* Warner Books, New York, 1999.

For the latest ISO Management Systems, see *https://www.iso.org/management-system-standards-list.html.*

Joseph Paris. *State of Readiness: Operational Excellence as Precursor to Becoming a High-Performance Organization.* Greenleaf Book Group, Austin, TX, 2017.

EPILOGUE

Robert K. Greenleaf. *The Servant as Leader.* Center for Applied Studies, Cambridge, MA, 1970.

Larry C. Spears. "Character and Servant Leadership: Ten Characteristics of Effective, Caring Leaders." *The Journal of Virtues and Leadership.* School of Global Leadership and Entrepreneurship, Regent University, Vol. 1, No. 1 (2010): pp. 25–30.

Larry C. Spears, ed. *Insights on Leadership: Service, Stewardship, Spirit, and Servant-leadership.* Wiley, New York, 1998.

Author

Brian Strobel has been leading people in operational environments for nearly 30 years. His initial academic pursuits trained him to be a physicist, but life had other plans. He's led large-scale military operations and led change across large companies. He's certified as a trainer for Situational Leadership, a Professional Coach, a Lean Six Sigma expert, and a Manager of Quality/Organizational Excellence.

He earned a Master's in Management and another in Executive Leadership, to include study under Ken Blanchard. His resume reveals a consultant, corporate executive, author, and Marine Officer, but resumes can fail to summarize what's important. A better summary relates that he strives to be a servant to those he leads.

Brian's path has been different than most, but always one focused on excellence. This path eventually revealed life's plan. He's now fully dedicated to this pursuit, living in the foothills of the Sierra Nevada with his wife and his new dog. When not helping others in the pursuit of excellence, you can find him with his wife and that dog enjoying the mountains.